Prai

HOUSE RULES

"In business, politics, religion, or the nonprofit sector, authentic leadership requires trust-based relationships. Anyone who fails to constantly build trust may become the 'boss,' but never the leader. Larry captures our need as leaders to first and foremost focus on the impacts of our decisions and actions on those we aspire to lead."

—**Ron Holifield,** Chief Executive Officer, Strategic Government Resources

"Larry James is the kind of leader I aspire to be: authentic and effective. He continues to grow and evolve to meet today's challenges. *House Rules* provides an inside look at Larry's journey as a leader while discerning core leadership principles that result in resilient, impactful teams. While *House Rules* is set in the complex, sometimes dangerous world of community development, the lessons are transferrable to any aspiring leader."

—**Carol Redmond Naughton,** President, Purpose Built Communities

"Many people genuinely want to help fight poverty. But there's a gap between wanting to see change and truly making change happen. Larry James's leadership is closing the gap. I learn everything I can from Larry."

—**Rev. Paul Rasmussen,** Senior Minister, Highland Park United Methodist Church

"*House Rules* is a compassionate, honestly lived, and warmly told account of Larry's twenty-five-year journey working with the poor in Dallas, both individually and systemically. The human stories, lessons learned, and questions raised are not only crucial to our national debate on rising inequality and shrinking resources, but also instructive to well-intended religious, civic, and business leaders."

—**J. McDonald Williams,** retired CEO of Trammell Crow Company, Founder and Chair of Foundation for Community Empowerment

"Without dismissing empirical research on effective leadership, Larry rightly emphasizes that, ultimately, leadership is an art. Larry captures insights that I emphasized in my forty years of teaching and consulting with executives, and he adds relevant principles that, based on my experience, ring true. His clear, refreshing style makes this book even more valuable as a resource for leadership development in any organization."

—**Jere E. Yates,** Professor Emeritus of Management, Pepperdine University

"Dallas is a better city because of the stellar leadership of Larry James. He skillfully leads with head, heart, and humility—a rare combination. I've always wondered what his secret was for such exceptional leadership. *House Rules* contains the essence of this leadership. Take this book and absorb it; you will be a better person and a better leader."

—**Bryan Carter,** Senior Pastor, Concord Church

"Larry James speaks words of wisdom and unity in our current world of polarity in politics, wealth distribution, and racial disparities. *House Rules* contains forty years of life lessons and leadership advice from a man who is not merely talking about change but living it."

—**Jeffrey Zsohar,** MD, Medical Director of Baylor Scott & White Community Care Clinics

"Every time I have the opportunity to talk with Larry James, I walk away with new leadership insight. This book is like a lifetime of visits with Larry, and it showcases how leadership, grounded in emotional intelligence, is in his humble bone marrow. The advice is practical, and the invitations for reflection helped me look at old dilemmas with fresh eyes."

—**Michelle Kinder,** Executive Director, Momentous Institute

"*House Rules* begins as a practical, honest guide for nonprofit leaders. It ends with the kind of philosophical and insightful approach to addressing poverty that could only come from Larry James."

—**Daniel Roby,** Executive Director, Austin Street Center

"If you are leading in city government, establishing a social enterprise, joining a movement, or raising kids in the city, there is something for you in this book. If you are doing all of the above, it is necessary reading. *House Rules* is one of those books that will become your companion. Go ahead and get two copies. You will want to share with someone you care about."

—**Liz Cedillo-Pereira,** Director, Office of Welcoming Communities & Immigrant Affairs, City of Dallas

HOUSE
RULES

HOUSE RULES

Insights for INNOVATIVE LEADERS

Best regards

LARRY M. JAMES

LEAFWOOD
PUBLISHERS
an imprint of Abilene Christian University Press

HOUSE RULES
Insights for Innovative Leaders

LEAFWOOD
P U B L I S H E R S
an imprint of Abilene Christian University Press

Copyright © 2018 by Larry M. James

ISBN 978-0-89112-422-1

Printed in the United States of America

Scripture quotations, unless otherwise noted, are from The Holy Bible, New International Version®, NIV®. Copyright © 1973, 1978, 1984, 2011 by Biblica, Inc.® Used by permission. All rights reserved worldwide.

Scripture quotations noted NRSV are taken from the New Revised Standard Version Bible, copyright © 1989, the Division of Christian Education of the National Council of the Churches of Christ in the United States of America. Used by permission. All rights reserved.

Cataloging-in-Publication Data is on file at the Library of Congress, Washington DC.

Cover design by Bruce Gore | Gore Studio, Inc.
Interior text design by Sandy Armstrong, Strong Design

Leafwood Publishers is an imprint of Abilene Christian University Press
ACU Box 29138
Abilene, Texas 79699

1-877-816-4455
www.leafwoodpublishers.com

18 19 20 21 22 23 / 7 6 5 4 3 2 1

Gladly remembering

Clyde and Bea Erwin
and
Morris and Mildred James

CONTENTS

ACKNOWLEDGMENTS

Nothing as complicated as telling a book-length story happens simply because one person sits down and writes. Certainly, that's not how this book came about. Truthfully, I've been working on this book for over four decades!

As for the book itself, I remain indebted to the wonderful folks at Leafwood Publishers who've made it all happen. Thanks, Duane, Rebecka, and Jason.

While I gladly accept all the responsibility for and any criticism of what you read here, not a word would have been possible without so many amazing people who've shown up to bless my life.

From that little, white church house situated between a soybean field and the woods in central Arkansas where I pastored during college; to a year-long stint in graduate school in Memphis, four years after Dr. King's tragic assassination; to a challenging and rather racist congregation in Shreveport, Louisiana; to the midtown church I served in wonderful New Orleans; to the special fourteen years I spent as senior minister of the church where I grew up in Richardson, Texas; to the powerful experience I enjoyed as a member of the Central Dallas Church located in the inner city of East Dallas; and, more recently, to the amazing congregation that is the Highland Park United Methodist Church—people constantly stepped into my life again and again to provide me exactly what I needed for each part of my journey.

The same amazing phenomenon continued as I moved, almost a quarter of a century ago and counting, to CitySquare. And now, for over a decade, my experience in becoming an ordained United Methodist elder in full connection with the North Texas Conference of the United Methodist Church has kept the inspiration flowing to my benefit. Bishop William Oden, Bishop Michael McKee, Dr. John Fiedler, Rev. Paul Rasmussen, the late Dr. Bill Bryan, Dr. Terry Parsons, Dr. Georg Rieger, Dr. Owen Ross, Dr. Zan Holmes, Dr. Sheron Patterson, Dr. Henry Masters, Rev. Richie Butler, Rev. Cammy Gaston, Dr. David Shawver, Rev. Preston Weaver, Rev. Katherine Glaze Lyle, Rev. Don Barnes, and so many others from the church affected my own understanding of leadership development and real service over the years.

Other extremely influential leaders in my own maturation include the minister of my earliest memory, the late Johnny Jackson, who exuded a quality of leadership shaped by pure love and kindness. Russell Herring, John Wood, Sheridan Umphress, Scotty English, Dr. Jerry Jones, Dr. Jimmy Allen, Dr. Jim Howard, Dr. James Cone, Dr. James Mosteller, Dr. John Boles, Dr. Richard Hughes, Randy Mayeux, Rev. Gerald Britt, Edd Eason, and John Greenan form just a portion of a long line of important people of great influence on me.

Of course, most of the considerations of this book developed and made themselves obvious to me at CitySquare. My continuing thanks to the entire CitySquare team—staff members, directors of our board, volunteers, and neighbors all! Among this wonderful group, Dan Hopkins deserves special note. Dan and I observed one another raising our families—quite the journey itself. In addition, Dan and I have endured one marathon in Alaska and over thirty years of friendship. As a volunteer with great expertise in construction and development, and a devoted donor, Dan helped us build CitySquare just because he cares about people, including me!

It was over a long breakfast conversation with Dave Shipley, chairman of the CitySquare board, and Kevin Thomason, CitySquare board member, that I began to sketch the outline of this book. Dave's counsel concerning thought connections moved me forward in this project. Dave has served CitySquare faithfully and with joy for over two decades. I'm fortunate to have such a friend.

At that same table over the last several years and still going, Kevin Thomason lends his considerable expertise and obvious devotion to CitySquare and to me. His frank feedback, as well as his commitment to compassion and justice, has carried me through good times and tough times, often without him even knowing it. The added benefit of his great trout-fishing excursions lifts my soul!

My special thanks to Dr. John Siburt, my dear friend, thought-partner, and successor. John's hunger for discovery, his intellectual curiosity, and his amazing ability to build and lead teams inspires me. John is wise far beyond his years. He serves as a model of effective, straightforward, servant leadership. Without even recognizing it, John motivated me to tackle this project. By stepping into the role of CitySquare president, he allowed me to stay on as chief executive officer. I'm grateful for him and for the many ways he has extended my work life. I've observed in John Siburt again and again the principles you read here.

None of my experiences among "the poor" in East and South Dallas would have ever occurred without the vision, generosity, patience, and continuing support of CitySquare founder Jim

Sowell. He is one of my deep friends. I know I can count on Jim for support and wise counsel, as well as creative input and valuable ideas. His leadership qualities and style instruct me in ways that he doesn't see. The influence he's had on my life and work can't be adequately expressed or fully understood. I will be forever indebted to Jim for the work he created for me and so many others to perform.

Of course, whatever worth or value one might discover in my life or in what life has taught me must be traced back to my family. My parents and grandparents on both sides of the family tree modeled honesty, directness, hard work, faith, grace, optimism, basic good humor, and love. They set a high bar; but when I failed to sail over it, they replaced it, helped me up, and cheered me on. I learned a great deal about leadership from each of them.

My wife, Brenda Erwin, traces her life's defining values back to the same sort of folks as mine. I've learned more than I can say about life, leadership, and love from her. Especially in the realms of patience, candor, wisdom, and good sense, Brenda has been my lifelong professor.

My daughters, their husbands, and my four wonderful grandchildren continue the saga, a truth for which I am so grateful. I always smile when I think of them, all clearly effective leaders along their own part of the trail. I could include stories of pure goodness and hope here that would embarrass them but inspire every reader. I resist in honor of their humility. Take it from me— they are such good, good people!

With so many tremendous people arrayed around me and numerous injustices conspiring to give me advantages over so many people on the planet, I consider myself a person of amazing privilege. I wrote *House Rules* in response to many questions— some from me; some from others. One question awaits an answer beyond this life: Why have I been so fortunate?

FOREWORD

I'm a firm believer in deep expertise—the kind that comes from a long effort, over the course of many years. What Friedrich Wilhelm Nietzsche called "a long obedience in the same direction." When you find such deep expertise in a person's life story and work, then that person is worth paying careful attention to.

Larry James is such a person.

I've known Larry for decades. We first met when we each served as ministers within the same denomination. I was preaching in Long Beach, California, and Larry was pastoring a church in Richardson, Texas (later in this book, you'll read about his work among people with AIDS in Richardson in the early days of that horrible disease). We were part of a group that met as the "Young Bucks of the Brotherhood." Well, we are no longer as young, and not in the same brotherhood. But our ties have lingered and deepened. As someone who knows the man behind this book well, here are a couple of things you might want to know about Larry.

First, he cares—genuinely, deeply, tangibly—for those in need. Pick your term: the poor, the dispossessed, the afflicted. These are the people he cares for. That care comes from a deep place within him, and it was most surely fed by numerous life experiences—life experiences that he chose. From choosing to play with neighborhood kids in New Orleans, where he was doing his graduate work and pastoring a church, to sitting on the front porch of an abandoned house in South Dallas with homeless folks, taking them ice water and enjoying the conversations, he learned from them and cherished the relationships he built.

Second, he is a successful leader. He is a leader with vision who has produced results—astonishing results, to be honest. I remember the precursor to CitySquare (the large nonprofit he leads). It was a storefront food pantry along Central Expressway, a few miles north of downtown Dallas. This effort was well-meaning, volunteer-based community support that provided food but not much else. When Larry was brought on to find better ways, and more ways, to lead this effort, it was as though he had been born, trained, and shaped to take on this challenge. That small, modest food pantry grew to more and more buildings, then additional services, and so on. Now, on a recent day when I visited the CitySquare Opportunity Center (you really should see this place), a group of well over one hundred business leaders from another major city were touring the place, trying to determine how they could do a better job in their city. My recommendation to that group is this: find a leader like Larry James and set that leader loose.

Let me add a third thing you should probably know about Larry. It's tough to describe, and it flows from the deep expertise I've tried to capture for you. He is comfortable with people, and he knows how to reach different kinds of people with his personal connections. Larry loves to sit on the front porch with a homeless man, learn from him, and cherish that relationship. Larry can also speak to business leaders alongside the mayor of Dallas, learn from those business leaders, and cherish those relationships.

This is no small ability.

This book is written by a talented leader, but it is also written by Larry the student, the life-long learner.

Why did he ask me to write this foreword? Partly because I read books for a living. I read and prepare synopses of at least two books each month for monthly "book clubs" in Dallas: the First Friday Book Synopsis and the Urban Engagement Book Club. I have done this for twenty years now: one business book and one social justice book each and every month. Larry thinks I know something about good books. And, I think Larry's book is one of those good books, worthy of your time.

This book is Larry saying, "This is what I've learned about leadership that I think is worth passing on to others."

He writes some of what he knows and some of what he has learned. He's learned things from reading books, and from leading an organization that is far larger than when he started. He did not take over at a large organization; he led a small organization and helped it grow. I've read enough business books to know just how impressive and rare that is—especially in the social justice/nonprofit arena in which he operates.

What will you find in this book? You will find seasoned advice for things leaders need to know and do—really listening to your clients; setting people free to make their own decisions and giving them permission (even encouraging them) to fail; dreaming, planning, scrambling, and foraging to find the next resource, the next dollar you need to accomplish that next step toward helping others.

Larry has also been at this long enough that you will find hints and suggestions about succession planning. How do you keep the dream going when it is time to let a new leader take over?

Of course, as the experts say, talk is cheap. So, don't miss this: Larry James knows how to execute. That's business speak for "Larry knows how to turn a dream into reality and keep it going, effectively, day after day, month after month, year after year—a little bigger, and at times a whole lot bigger, as time marches on."

Here's a special insight that I think Larry is uniquely qualified to offer. Chapter Three of this book is titled "Honor Tradition; Celebrate Innovation." This requires two elements. First, you have to know the traditions that you will honor. This former pastor knows plenty about such traditions. Second, you have to develop the ability to innovate. Larry has done just that, in very noticeable ways!

He has even developed expertise he never knew he needed, like medical treatment expertise (CitySquare has done groundbreaking work for people with diabetes) and real estate expertise (CitySquare has provided homes for hundreds of the formerly homeless and those in need of affordable housing). As I said, Larry is a genuine, life-long learner.

So, if you lead any kind of organization, or any group of people, this book is for you.

One line from this book to remember during your day-to-day struggles: "Never quitting matters, and it matters a lot."

Leaders don't quit. They really don't. Larry hasn't ever quit, and that matters. He learns; he listens; he leads; he never quits.

This book might help you decide not to quit either.

Randy Mayeux
Dallas, Texas

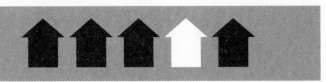

PREFACE

For me, leadership is more art than science.

No doubt, I'll have some strong pushback on that perspective. I'm aware of the various management theories and approaches that have been studied and evaluated scientifically. I get the fact that all sorts of useful resources have been developed to measure skills, aptitude, personality types, and leadership styles. And I've found that much of that body of work is extremely helpful. My teams have been exposed to much of this learning. We've taken full advantage of the tools available that feel rooted in a measure of predictability and precise scientific inquiry. We will continue to do so. Leaders understand the science beneath their effectiveness. Effective leaders engage the scientific side of their craft. As a result, they and their teams grow in productivity, relevance, efficiency, harmony, self-understanding, cultural sensitivity, and real-time value.

At the same time, experienced leaders understand that compelling leadership is also a true art form. Nuance, grace, human connection, creativity, spiritual depth, and a commitment to mission that is shaped primarily by love and dedication—these "softer," more subjective dimensions of leadership make it clear that good and great leaders practice their craft as artists.

My art-science metaphor might be inadequate. The scientist in me retreats almost naturally to the clarity of tests, measurements, outcomes, and other tools born of the laboratory approach. However, life rushes in on my experience and people have a way of showing up.

People break hearts.

People conquer overwhelming odds.

People long to be better, do better, and achieve more.

People win because they are winners by nature.

People hurt and heal.

People issues drive me toward the artistic side of my own inner life, as well as into my work as a leader.

So as people arrive, I'm drawn back to the studio, palette before me and brush in hand, to try one more time to get it right: to tell a story, paint a picture, capture a photograph, sing a song, or write a poem.

Leadership at its best is truly a fascinating art form.

So I write.

To be honest, I hate this impulse I can't seem to shake. Somehow, it's as if I am forced to write. There remains this almost inexplicable need to get out what I think I've learned. I find myself caught between the palpable desire to escape into quiet and silence where I may rest, unperturbed, subject to no review or question, and the absolute obligation to stand up as a witness to testify concerning the truth I've been blessed to discover and to experience.

At the moment of decision to risk writing, I realize once again that leadership is a spiritual experience for both leader and those led. Deeply rooted in the belief that people forever remain the highest priority for the true leader, practicing the art of leadership occurs in the realm of the Spirit. Leadership that results in significant accomplishments possesses powerful access to often unrecognized but universal spiritual dimensions.

Real leaders walk in and with a discernable "spirit."

What I have in mind here is born not so much of a religion or any particular religious tradition but of a human reservoir of universal spirituality. Everyone arrives in life with what I have in mind here. But this spirit can be illusive. This force calls for discovery. Its mystery surprises us. Often indefinable, this spirit is breath and soul and heart and creative force behind, over, and within all great leaders. While we struggle to comprehend or define it, we all know this spirit when we see it or encounter it. Efforts that attempt to create or instill it don't work well. About all one can do to engage or receive this unexplored dimension is to *live open*.

Not long ago, as I was pulling out of our parking lot, I spotted one of our executive leaders here at CitySquare. She is extremely intelligent, well qualified for her position, and off-the-charts creative. But what I observed perfectly captured this notion of leading and living "in the Spirit." I watched as she cleared the seat in her van to make a place for an older gentleman. The man lived on the streets with a serious set of disabilities. He needed something to eat and a ride to a particular destination in the neighborhood.

Her work that day could not be found as a part of her position description.

It is what she does.

It reflects who she is.

Her action told me so clearly, "I'm on mission, and I'm really sorry you noticed!" This is living in the Spirit.

Again and again, I've watched as people realize that this Spirit is their greatest asset to fully embrace our house rules, to say nothing of the fullness of a life lived in this mission. Authentic leaders lead from a place far beyond ego games. Effective leaders recognize the inherent waste that occurs when engaging in such foolish exercises. Ego-based attempts at leadership eventually reveal themselves to be ineffective at best and the source of a deadly, nonproductive pathology at worst.

The authentic leader realizes that the people she leads deserve the very best. Great leaders find creative ways to bring people and teams along so that great things result. Great leaders rally their troops, drawing on unexpected strength and surprising visions that emerge from the deepest places within themselves and everyone involved.

I Write Because of What I Know about Great Leaders

Great leaders inspire great joy.

Great leaders celebrate the goodness discovered in their
    team members.

Great leaders often hope against great, seemingly insurmountable odds; and then, they rise up and provide exactly what their teams require to achieve success.

Great leaders create.

Great leaders find ways to prepare team members for increased responsibility and personal advancement within their organizations and even beyond, out in the sector or field of their endeavors.

Great leaders empower those who follow them.

Great leaders model absolute honesty.

Great leaders believe in goodness as they face great difficulty.

Great leaders possess amazing heart.

Great leaders know how to fail with tremendous grace.

Great leaders rise again after a fall or failure.

Great leaders know that the number of times one fails doesn't matter, since, as Dallas Mavericks' owner Mark Cuban said in a speech to students, "you only have to succeed once!"

Great leaders embrace responsibility, while sharing all credit with those they lead when credit shows up to be shared.

Great leaders act out unquestioned humility.

Great leaders value others above themselves for the good of the team and the success of the mission.

Great leaders take the blame, but deflect the fame.

Great leaders exhibit an inspiring fearlessness.

Great leaders remain open to big visions, no matter how seemingly foolish or grandiose.

Great leaders are dreamers.

Great leaders know what it means to be considered unrealistic and impractical.

Great leaders enjoy meeting new people.

Great leaders may not like meetings but take them daily for the good of the team and another chance to explore unthinkable possibilities.

Great leaders unflinchingly pursue justice.

Great leaders abhor racism and hatred and never tolerate them in their organizations or their team members.

Great leaders see things differently most of the time.

Great leaders operate out of a fundamental commitment to fairness.

Great leaders exhibit delightful curiosity about almost everything.

Great leaders arrive at surprising conclusions that more often than not result in unexpected progress.

Great leaders pursue learning with enthusiasm.

Great leaders read constantly.

Great leaders move through life and their organizations with a
calm confidence, as if they know something no one else sees
or understands.

Great leaders pursue life-long learning.

Great leaders confess their failures and their faults.

Great leaders love people.

Great leaders see beyond the failings of others.

Great leaders display surprising tenderness in the context of
unflinching strength.

Great leaders care about those who follow. This care is personal.

Great leaders seek to know their team members—family, interests, hobbies, dreams, life goals, skills, history, failures,
and disappointments.

Great leaders display comfort in the board room, on the front
line, or at a coffee table.

Great leaders never expect deference, credit, or special treatment
because they continuously extend all three.

Great leaders hold their teams to standards of exceptional
performance because they first hold themselves to the
same standards.

Great leaders look for ways to honor and encourage others.

Great leaders possess passion for the mission, and no one on the
team ever doubts it.

Great leaders love catching their team members in the act of
doing something great.

Great leaders provide for the health and balance of those
they lead.

Great leaders serve as their team's constant guide toward the
organization's true North Star.

Great leaders find ways to retreat into reflection and quiet.

Great leaders meditate.

Great leaders value the inner life and make sufficient provision
for its health and development.

Great leaders inspire confidence.

Great leaders are approachable.

Great leaders, as I said, walk in the Spirit. As a result, great leaders convey that same knowing ability to those who follow.

House Rules draws deeply on my experience as a leader at CitySquare, a broad-ranging, poverty-fighting nonprofit organization at work in inner city Dallas, with a presence in other Texas cities, including Fort Worth, Waco, Kaufman, Paris, Austin, and Houston, as well as in Denver, Colorado. Being a part of the CitySquare team has been the highlight of my professional life. Much of what follows describes many of the unique challenges I've faced while working in this truly wonderful organization.

The house rules at CitySquare always intend to honor neighbors, care for every team member, and change the city for the good of everyone.

That takes leadership.

But I believe more strongly than ever that what I've learned here can be applied anywhere people come together around an agreed-upon mission. Whether you manufacture widgets or work for justice, leadership will be required and called for. Each chapter of *House Rules* includes a "Your Turn" exercise. You may want to use these sections as a journaling opportunity to record your reflections. Or, you may want to involve your team members or associates in a group exercise as you read *House Rules* together. I wrote *House Rules* with you in mind and for your personal consideration as a leader.

CHAPTER ONE

LET PEOPLE FAIL

I suppose it is hardest for parents.

Something churns up from deep within any time a parent feels as if her child might fail. A built-in instinct drives a parent to rush forward in full rescue mode at the first hint of danger or peril. Protecting a child, buffering the blows that threaten to hurt, harm, or set back a child—well, it is just what parents do.

But good parents do so selectively and on a limited basis. That is because failure is an important part of life and growing up. Few teachers can match the learning outcomes of simple, every-day failure.

Effective team leaders don't treat people they lead like their children. But some of the same instincts surface whenever leaders perceive that failure lurks as a real possibility for the team or for individual team members.

I've noticed across the years that those leaders who rush in to protect their charges act out of fear. Often, that fear is motivated by the leader's self-interest. Failure must be avoided at all costs to protect the image or reputation of the leader. Thankfully, strong leaders find ways to move beyond this natural inclination to protect personal image or avoid blame, even at the expense of those whom they lead.

Still, every leader knows the sinking feeling accompanying reports of possible or fully realized failure. Fear often gives way to premature interventions on failed efforts. These reactions are totally understandable.

When I see failure headed my way, I often do all that I can to regain or maintain some level of control to avert a negative outcome. Effective leaders realize the importance of taking the long view when it comes to team outcomes or the performance of individual team members.

I like what Parker Palmer says about leaders who disseminate light:

> If leaders are to cast less shadow and more light, we
> need to ride certain monsters all the way down,
> explore the shadows they create, and experience the
> transformation that can come as we "get into" our
> spiritual lives. . . . The best leaders in every setting
> reward people for taking worthwhile risks even if they
> are likely to fail. These leaders know that the death of an
> initiative . . . is always a source of new learning.[1]

Clearly, experiencing failure opens opportunity for the growth and emergence of courage. Without failure and overcoming it, courage remains stunted.

Fear Breeds Control

Excessively controlling leaders undermine growth, discourage experimentation, and shut down innovation. A leader who obsesses on fear of failure often creates a culture of control that gives way to micromanagement and overreaching leadership behaviors. When leaders overreach, talent is wasted and progress stalls.

One of the most important lessons a leader must learn is that failure is seldom fatal! In fact, failure, if handled properly, leads to growth, personal development, team strength, and essential learning. Providing team members with the freedom to fail, as well as the appropriate follow-up support after failure, opens new avenues for growth, leadership development, and enhanced understanding of any challenge or problem. The flourishing of an entrepreneurial spirit of pioneering discovery occurs only in an environment of trust where failure is not only allowed but expected. Responding creatively to failure represents one of the most promising opportunities an effective leader will ever encounter. Sadly, impatient, controlling leaders too often fail to capitalize on the unique opportunity offered by looming or accomplished failure.

Several years ago, our team included one of the brightest young leaders I've ever known. He led one of our most essential teams. At a crucial juncture in our annual work plan, he allowed his inflated self-confidence to override his better judgment in dealing with a vital opportunity and its rapidly approaching deadline. Rebuffing team members' offers to assist him in any way possible, he kept to his plan. Unfortunately, he badly miscalculated the time needed to meet his project deadline. He missed his goal. His failure cost our organization dearly.

What would you have done?

Of course, no one felt worse about this clear failure than did he. He acknowledged to me that his own pride clouded his decision not to allow other team members to assist him. He offered his resignation. He invited me to fire him.

I refused. Why?

Here was a great young person with virtually unlimited potential and ability. The short-term play appeared obvious: terminate and document! But a longer view took into account an understanding of the inevitability and necessity of failure. This understanding provided the space I needed to work with him. First, I talked him off the professional ledge of career suicide! Next, we confronted his error in great detail. Then, we moved forward *together*, recognizing that his best days were ahead for both him and CitySquare. Part of the moving forward involved him creating a clear plan for addressing future situations like the one in which he had failed so miserably. Beyond the immediate failure, we also set up a "coaching" conversation with some built-in accountabilities we both agreed on. In the process, I owned the failure. After all, he played on my team, the only team for which I am responsible. The failure was as much mine as his, actually more mine. My decision turned out to be the right one. He served the organization well until he left to take a better job with more responsibility. Since that failure, he successfully built a great employment record and is an effective leader in his own right. We stay in touch and respect and admire each other greatly. I regard embracing his failure as an investment in his life and in the good of our community. He has not let me down nor proven my action foolhardy. And, you know, it's not about me anyway!

Expecting Failure as Part of Your Culture

For years, I've communicated to my teams that if they aren't failing, they aren't trying hard enough, thinking big enough, or risking significantly enough. If exploration and innovation come at the price of the real risk of failure, then failure must be expected, encouraged, tolerated, and celebrated. Moments of crushing failure often turn out to be crucial steps on the way to huge breakthroughs. Failure provides determined change agents the training most needed for future success. Incidents of failure should be seen as stepping stones on the pathway of adventure, learning, and dynamic discovery.

Upon his successful invention of the light bulb, Thomas Edison was asked by a reporter how it felt to "fail 1,000 times" before achieving success. Edison is reported to have replied, "I didn't fail 1,000 times. The light bulb was an invention with 1,000 steps."[2] On another occasion, Edison commented, "I make more mistakes than anyone I know. And eventually I patent them."[3]

Leaders identify capable people to join their teams. If we are smart, we will seriously consider hiring new employees who readily admit past failures, especially if such prospects can link failure to progress and newly discovered innovation. Once on board, effective leaders clarify the mission, lay out the expectations, define the challenges as currently understood, provide support, and then, most importantly, let their people operate on their own or in teams that enjoy freedom and authority to execute, innovate, experiment, and create. Leaders can't encourage growth or experience team breakthroughs without a level of confidence and security to simply let people operate out of their own initiative and judgment. From the first day on the job, if I cannot trust a team member with the expected possibility of failure as he goes about his responsibilities, I should not have hired him.

Effective leaders discover ways to grow their people. These leaders realize that failure on the part of a team member or an entire team most often is not a negative reflection on leadership ability. In fact, failure and its management may provide evidence of stellar leadership capacity. How leaders respond to failure will be crucial for team growth and long-term success as a unit of change and productivity.

Leaders who curtail or limit their teams, especially out of a fear of failure, guarantee limited results. The leader who fears failure and who makes decisions primarily out of that fearfulness consigns his entire team to mediocre results.

Fear of failure can chain a leader to a catwalk above his team, so that the leader's time is wasted watching "trusted" team members rather than spending precious time imagining the next phases and stages of the team vision. The leader preoccupied with a fear of failure ensures limited results. She creates an organization replete with formidable barriers, demoralized employees, few options, and unrecognized opportunities.

The over-critical eye of the leader focused on failure dooms a team to frustration, disillusionment, and defeat. Creating an organizational culture that expects and absorbs failure provides the space needed to realize success and real effectiveness.

Learning to Admit and Own Failure

Organizations possessing a healthy respect for and expectation of failure enjoy an atmosphere in which failure can be readily admitted. Effective leaders make sure that their team members not only feel free to own up to their own failures, but they create formal venues for discussing and analyzing failed attempts at hitting agreed-upon targets. Effective leaders model this behavior so that those whom they lead will understand that talking about failure is not only acceptable, it is part of the work process of the dynamic organization of which they are an essential member. Organizations in which failure can be admitted, discussed honestly, and evaluated by trusted team members will minimize fault-finding and blame games, both counterproductive actions that sap a group of its life and collective effectiveness. If I realize that I can face my failure with transparency and realistically expect support from those around me, my productivity can be enhanced by my failures.

By the way, leaders fail, too. Leaders model the appropriate response to failure by admitting their own mistakes as they occur. Every leader worth his salt will fail. Often, a leader's failure takes place in public, in front of God and everyone! Other failures turn out to be more discreet. When the leader fails, no matter what the circumstances, he must admit it and submit to the same analysis and reflection as he expects whenever other team members fail. In fact, the failure of a leader usually provides a great opportunity for growth—growth of the leader and growth in understanding and appreciation by those who follow and observe. My experience in confronting and admitting my own failures tells me that "coming clean" about bad decisions and less-than-wise choices is always the right thing to do for me and my team.

Navy SEAL Leif Babin's summation about leaders and failure is on target:

> We are by no means infallible leaders; no one is, no
> matter how experienced. Nor do we have all the
> answers; no leader does. We've made huge mistakes.
> Often our mistakes provided the greatest lessons,
> humbled us and enabled us to grow and become better.
> For leaders, the humility to admit and own mistakes and
> develop a plan to overcome them is essential to success.
> The best leaders are not driven by ego or personal
> agendas. They are simply focused on the mission and
> how best to accomplish it.[4]

Real estate deals tend to be loaded with all sorts of land mines that explode in a multicolor canopy of failure! If the real estate project involves housing for working families or for the extremely poor, you can expect the potential failure factor to be multiplied many times over. Typically, cash is short, equity doesn't exist, and developers must beg and/or depend on public sources to build their capital stacks for development projects. In every one of the complicated development deals in which I've been involved, we've failed in one way or another, and often our failures in the same transaction have been numerous.

In each of these cases when failure came, we circled the wagons, evaluated our missteps, laughed about some aspects of our failures and erroneous assumptions, and then we went to work correcting the mistakes while formulating a new and better plan of attack. In every instance, if we allowed fear of failure to carry the day, we never would have developed a single unit of housing. We've had some surprising successes simply because we don't allow fear of failure to call the shots in our enterprise.

To pretend that failure will not occur is a cruel act to embrace. The prospect of failure follows any effort of real significance. Developing housing for people who don't enjoy the benefit of a home due to financial limitations and realities will be risky by definition. However, risking failure is worth it because of the definite upside resulting from success, even after many missteps.

Growth Results in "Leadership Ignorance"

One thing I know for certain: providing effective leadership is tough stuff!

To get things done, the leader must depend on others. That is a universal truth. If, as a leader, I know and understand everything that my organization is doing, then, clearly, we aren't doing enough, nor are we operating at full capacity! Effective organizations don't limit themselves by informing the boss of all that is going on.

Here's a very discomforting, counterintuitive leadership truth: as organizations grow, more and more of the decision-making, as well as the hard work, must be spread out "beneath" the leader (for more about top-down leadership, see Chapter Fifteen). As an organization grows in size and complexity and scope of work product, the leader must release more and more of her previous responsibilities and understandings to others. In a very real sense in growing organizations, the role of the leader must shrink while team members grow and increase in importance. One of the most threatening aspects of organizational growth is the fact that the leader's intimate, detailed knowledge of the various functions, products, and processes of his team diminish in direct proportion to company growth.

As a leader rises to more and more organizational and visionary responsibility, technical competency declines. Effective leaders must rely on others for knowledge and the answers to daily questions concerning the details, nuances, contingencies, and missional relationship of various decisions and functions. To create such dynamic, trusting, creative workplaces, leaders must cast aside inordinate fear of failure. The trust necessary to grow effective, highly functional organizations means that fear must be placed in proper perspective.

Risk aversion does not combine well with effective, world-changing leadership. As a leader, the only way to avoid destabilizing failure is to place your trust in the team you lead.

Principles to Consider

So how do we lead fearlessly while creating teams and organizations that function without fear of failure? How do we lead complex organizations whose success depends on our own diminishing understanding of some essential aspects of our work product?

Spread Decision-Making across Your Organization

Regardless of the size or history of your team, bring members inside the decision-makers' circle. Diversity here is always a plus. Learn to listen. No other leadership skill is more important than an authentic commitment to listen and to hear your team, your customers, and your critics. Communicate that failure won't doom the team or surprise anyone.

Set an expectation that failure is welcomed if it is the result of high-performing effort and commitment to mission realization and mission-advancing innovation. Let everyone own the mission and the organization.

When Failure Shows Up, and It Will, Support the Team Members Involved

Failure can be managed most effectively when surrounded by an authentically supportive team. Consequently, great leaders accept blame for team failures. They also give credit to others for success and breakthroughs. Telling a team and individual team members (and meaning it) "I have your back when you fail" will set people free for great work if, as a leader, you make good on such promises when failure occurs. Throwing a party for team success and spreading the accolades all around, with no thought of taking credit yourself, deepens team loyalty and provides motivation for more and more organizational success.

Hire Smart

I never want to hire someone who isn't smarter than me. To accomplish your mission, you must build a team that is smart enough to embrace risking failure with little or no thought of defeat. Expert people will make expert decisions. And, if supported by courageous leaders who dedicate themselves to providing protection and security, the successes of your team members will easily outpace their creative blunders! As with most dimensions of effective leadership, your job is to possess a thorough understanding of the risk of failure, but then to go forward and bet on the net upside of team performance.

Learn to Coach Your Team

Good coaches work at their craft continuously, even when things are moving along just as anticipated. Great coaches provide ongoing guidance. Effective coaches build in team time for reflection. Any coach expecting success, even in the face of setbacks, offers up "practice sessions" built around potential, real-life scenarios and cases. Great coaches spend the time necessary to get to know their teams and the individuals on those teams. Every team member will be different and motivated to work hard by numerous, unique factors. Coaches who get the most out of their teams engage their players at a deep, personal level. Phil Jackson, famed National Basketball Association head coach, reports an interesting habit he developed while coaching the world champion Chicago Bulls.

> My approach was subtle. Every year the team went on a long West Coast road trip in November when the circus took over the stadium for a few weeks. Before the trip I would select a book for each of the players to read, based on what I knew about them. . . . Some players read every book I gave them; others dumped them in the trash. But I never expected everyone's 100 percent engagement. The message I wanted to convey was that I cared enough about them as individuals to spend time searching for a book that might have special meaning for them. Or at least make them laugh.[5]

No wonder Jackson won so many rings!

Whenever, Wherever, If at All Possible, Fail Fast!

Once failure arrives and is recognized, stop! Admit the time for a reset has arrived. Take action immediately to change course, revamp, and/or shut down. More harmful than failure is any reluctance to call it out, and then to do something different. Failure will not be fatal unless we refuse to see it for what it is. Or worse, pretend that the results before us are the best we can do. If a leader and her team are going down one path and recognize that they are going the wrong way, their only smart choice is to stop and go back the way they came. Failure should never be considered permanent, but it must always be dealt with as quickly as possible for that assessment to prove true.

Establish the Clear Limits of Failure

Effective leaders recognize that some categories of failure always remain unacceptable and are not to be tolerated. Failure that compromises or challenges your clear, bedrock organizational values cannot be overlooked or ignored. Across the years in the settings where I've worked, we've experienced the personal implosion of a small number of team members who failed because they brought their unattended, untreated pathologies to the workplace. I can count them on one hand with fingers to spare. Still, the nature of our work among low-income people, already challenged and let down by individuals, institutions, and organizations all around, does not allow us to tolerate ethical failure. Failure that negatively affects the needs, desires, and expectations of your customers must never be considered acceptable.

At times, a leader's loyalty to team members can backfire, resulting in damage to team morale, as well as erosion of trust in team leadership. Occasionally, my understanding of team leadership results in my "hanging with" an ineffective team member for longer than I should for my own sake, the failing team member's professional good, and my team's benefit. I've learned the hard way that a crucial part of team formation, sustainability, and effectiveness will involve me listening carefully to team members at every level of the organization. Frankly, from a pragmatic standpoint, a high-producing employee who makes life easy for upper-level leaders can at times be wreaking havoc among other frontline team members in the organization. Even when reports of challenges reach high-level leaders, the temptation will be to maintain the status quo in light of positive performance metrics. While the temptation to stay the course may be understandable, in every case I've experienced, such a decision is simply not sustainable. Failure turns unacceptable when it threatens the health and well-being of other team members. The reluctance of team leaders to deal with such inappropriate actions spreads a poison throughout the organization, and sooner or later the negative results can be dramatic.

Quickly Address Any Failure That Hurts Other Team Members

Mistakes of this sort must be corrected immediately upon recognition. Losing the respect of fellow team members, a community, or a constituency can threaten the viability and purpose of the whole organization. Failure along these crucial, life-giving boundaries must be met with transparency, complete honesty, and a strong commitment to correct the detrimental impact of this sort of failure as quickly as possible. Systems failure puts all hands on deck to correct the consequences of and the injury caused by any such failure as completely as possible for everyone involved.

My natural tendency or default response to everyone on my teams has been to see the positive in everyone and to focus on the strengths people bring to their work. As a general rule, this works well—until it doesn't.

Not long ago, two of our most productive leaders shared a conversation about this characteristic of mine to always see the upside in others.

"Larry sees the good in everyone," one friend observed. "And, at times that comes back to hurt him, and occasionally the rest of us." The other fellow agreed, but then added, "That likely explains why the two of us are here!" My first friend agreed with a laugh, and later they reported the exchange to me.

Failure doesn't feel good. Instinctively, almost everyone works hard to avoid failure. Honestly, though, most of my fear of failure places too much emphasis on me as the leader. Managing failure in a productive manner is not about me at all.

It's all about the team. It's the stuff of leadership development. Reacting to it properly is a large part of how we get our stuff done. The prayer of Rabindranath Tagore, "The Grasp of Your Hand," moves me deeply as I consider my own ever-present failures:

> Let me not pray to be sheltered from dangers,
> but to be fearless in facing them.
> Let me not beg for the stilling of my pain, but
> for the heart to conquer it.
> Let me not crave in anxious fear to be saved,
> but hope for the patience to win my freedom.
> Grant me that I may not be a coward, feeling
> Your mercy in my success alone; but let me find
> the grasp of Your hand in my failure.[6]

Your Turn

1. Think about a time when you failed. What did you need most in the midst of that experience? Why? How did the experience affect you? Did you come out of it feeling positive or negative? Why?
2. Now recall a time when a team you were a part of or were leading failed. How did you react to the failure? What did your team need? If you were a leader at the time, how did you feel? What did you do? Were you satisfied with the outcome?

What did you learn? What could you have done differently or better?

3. Do you believe failure can be a good thing? Why or why not?

4. When you fail or when your team fails, do you take it personally? Explain.

5. As a leader, have you ever allowed a person who failed in violation of your values to remain on your team or to go unaddressed? Spend a few moments reflecting on that experience. What did you learn? How did you resolve the situation? How did your team react to the failure and to your handling of it?

6. The next time you experience failure, what, if anything, will you do differently?

NOTES

[1] Parker J. Palmer, *Let Your Life Speak: Listening for the Voice of Vocation* (San Francisco: Jossey-Bass, 1999), Kindle.

[2] Pauline Estrem, "Why Failure Is Good for Success," *Success*, August 25, 2016, https://www.success.com/article/why-failure-is-good-for-success.

[3] Christopher Gergen and Gregg Vanourek, "The Value of Failure," *Harvard Business Review*, October 2, 2008, https://hbr.org/2008/10/the-value-of-failure.

[4] Jocko Willink and Leif Babin, *Extreme Ownership: How U.S. Navy SEALs Lead and Win* (New York: St. Martin's Press, 2015), 8.

[5] Phil Jackson, *Eleven Rings: The Soul of Success* (New York: Penguin, 2013), 126.

[6] Rabindranath Tagore, *The Heart of God: Prayers of Rabindranath Tagore*, ed. Herbert Vetter (North Clarendon, VT: Tuttle Publishing, 1997), 39.

CHAPTER TWO

BREAKTHROUGHS FOLLOW DARKNESS

Significant change that results in progress always involves struggle and some measure of conflict. Almost always, difficulty precedes success. Power differentials, especially in the social sector, never shift without struggle and a real challenge to existing social structures. Darkness and opposition are part of the game. I expect this truth is lost on no one.

I witness this reality every day where I work.

Poor people know the darkness of which I speak. Watching the working poor and the homeless provides keen insights into the processes and prospects of achieving life-changing progress and success. Life is not fair. Some must battle harder and longer than others to rise to new levels of life experience and accomplishment. But I've learned from my financially impoverished friends that courage in the face of long odds pays off.

Never quitting matters, and it matters a lot.

A Friend's Struggle

Until a few months ago, my friend "Blue" lived on the streets of South Dallas. His life fell into a death spiral when his wife died after an extended illness. Blue fell apart. The darkness overwhelmed him. He became lost in chronic inebriation and homelessness. Blue was an exceptional thinker. I became acquainted with him while engaging homeless people on the street. My meager efforts involved passing out bottled water, hot coffee, and conversation. It was during this activity that Blue and I became friends. He told me his story more than once. But Blue lived in the darkness. He knew something better was on "the other side" of where he lived, but he couldn't determine how to get there in his grief.

He decided to keep trying.

Blue is brilliant. He has gifts to be taken seriously.

One afternoon, I sat down beside him on the steps leading from the sidewalk up to an abandoned, old house. He was reading a book.

When I asked him what he was reading, he handed me the book and asked me to read a passage, which I did. Profound, spiritual insights rolled off the pages of Blue's book and right into my heart. When I looked at the cover, I realized Blue had handed me Thomas Merton's *Thoughts in Solitude*. Blue found himself in a place of deep darkness, but he refused to remain or give up there.

Then, things got much worse.

I believe it was on a Wednesday afternoon, possibly Thursday.

Blue stepped off the curb onto Malcolm X Boulevard just as a speeding car raced down the street. The driver tried to avert hitting him but failed.

Blue's back and leg were crushed. He was rushed to a nearby hospital where he was admitted. Thankfully, he survived, but now in even deeper darkness. Over the following weekend, the hospital discharged Blue, who had no insurance. He ended up in the back of a friend's van. When we found him on Monday, he was lying in the back of the van on top of three mattresses trying to get better. Immediately, we took him to the Salvation Army where he secured a respite bed for a time of recovery. Thank God for our friends at the Salvation Army!

Blue persisted.

Blue battled.

Today, Blue has housing, thanks to several good friends.

Blue broke through in spite of the darkness. Today, Blue is running toward the light. It almost seems as if the darkness, the unknowing time, played a key role in the breakthrough at last. Like me, Blue's struggle is not done, but Blue knows the light and its goodness.

The "Progress Tunnel"

Great social movements in the United States reflect the truth about the necessity of struggle and a measure of turmoil and confusion. To recall the power and transformational heroics of the brave, socially innovative actors in the yet-unfinished civil rights movement is to be confronted with an historic parade of men and women who knew well the dynamic connection between struggle and progress. Many paid the ultimate price to advance their propositions. All knew difficulty firsthand.

Here's an idea for some personal growth time in understanding the connection between progress and struggle—spend a few minutes each morning for the next few weeks searching online for information on these exceptional people:

The family of Emmett Till, especially his mother, Mamie Till
Rosa Parks
Medgar Evers
Malcolm X

James Lawson
C. T. Vivian
John Lewis
Diane Nash
Bernard Lafayette
James Bevel
Martin Luther King Jr.

Or a more comprehensive approach might be to read in depth about more people shaped by struggle. To that end, consider making David Halberstam's classic *The Children* your bible for the next month.[1] Get ready though. You will learn about paying the price in an important "values transaction" needed to accomplish your most meaningful objectives. Be prepared to be tested as you move forward.

Often, progress is born out of dark times. The reward received upon emerging from the tunnel of darkness into a new day of light and clarity will make whatever sacrifice required well worth the struggle. It just helps to shape expectations and to count the cost before embarking.

What's true of individual advancement in basic human rights can also be true when it comes to organizational progress and reordering. Transforming organizations can be painful. Change usually involves a journey through doubt, pain, sacrifice, insecurity, and unknown territory. Those who understand and practice the fine art of simply going on usually turn out to be successful in their endeavors to bring transformation to the groups of people they lead or with whom they are associated.

It is just the truth: folks who understand the value of keeping on the path, even when it leads into a dark passage, are the people who succeed while so many others fall behind, drop out, and fail. When in the darkness, faith, if engaged, pushes you on in spite of doubt, fear, and opposition. Persistence prevails. Leadership forms in the crucible of struggle. Battling against long odds refines the soul, clarifies vision, and strengthens the heart. It's almost as if people who get important things done must experience the proving ground or a personal or group experience of passage through the dark tunnel. Leaders refined by struggle with the dark, hard times are leaders who battle on, no matter what the cost or the obstacles.

Organizations Resist Change

No matter how innovative or cutting edge, most organizations reach a point where they long for holding out against any more change. Truly great organizations go beyond the status quo and choose the option of continuing to grow, evolve, and improve. Such organizations turn out to be in a decided minority!

Lots of factors conspire to produce status quo-seeking organizational philosophies. Some of the factors contributing to organizational paralysis include

- satisfaction with what has been discovered and implemented
- safety that emerges from knowing the familiar and an unwillingness to jettison any tactics that maintain the comforts of doing what's always been done
- security in the established rules and regulations that block progress toward a better way of (you fill in the blank)
- sightlines aimed backward into the past

You name the organization—churches, civic clubs, schools, nonprofits, neighborhood groups, sports teams, businesses, political parties.

A commonly adopted reaction to time in the tunnel ahead is to hunker down and simply resist. Instinctively, we hang on to what we know. One of the keys to surviving the struggle and the darkness of the tunnel for any group has to do with its commitment to organizational values, the headlamps for organizational spelunkers! Clarity about the uncontested values of the group provides the light needed to move through any struggle. Organizations suffering from blurred or timid values cannot survive the tunnel.

Playing football in high school and college was one of the most formative experiences of my life. I remember well the toughness of the game. One of my line coach's favorite drills in high school was known as the "Eagle Blood Pit." Blocking dummies were aligned in such a way that they formed a tunnel of sorts with a player on each end. The goal of the drill was to prevail against your teammate, who would hurdle toward you from the opposite end of the tunnel. The objective was to push the other guy out of the back of the "pit."

When I visited Tulane University to investigate a football scholarship offer after high school, I found the same sort of setup, but at Tulane, the coaches replaced the open pit with a literal tunnel. In the college drill, you stayed in the tunnel until you drove your opponent out of the other end of the enclosed passageway. You may have faced multiple adversaries in the drill before you found escape from the pit. The only way out was through the harshness of the experience.

Life can be exactly like that.

Breakthroughs follow darkness.

Principles to Consider

Moving through the trauma, and sometimes the drama, of change necessitates reliance on and the application of dependable tools for managing difficult and dark times as a team. Here are a few of the guidelines or warnings as you move through times of struggle and uncertainty.

Expect to experience struggle and darkness if you are up to anything worthwhile.

Anything you can expect or realistically predict, you can prepare for—at least in part. When you confront struggles, regard them as the cost of doing business in your field of work. Without struggles or challenges, there will be no progress.

Regard struggles as vital endorsements of your mission.

If you never face challenging times, this absence of pain and discomfort should be evaluated. Honest reflection could lead you to reconsider your mission, to question the value of what it is you are attempting to do. On the other hand, when you face opposition and obstacles, take time to evaluate just how your challenges may be the indicator you need to keep moving forward. Again, roadblocks often signify you're headed in exactly the hard, difficult direction that current circumstances demand.

Be ready to encourage your teammates along the way as the struggle begins, intensifies, and tops out.

Be clear about how you regard challenges. Interpret the negative experiences in positive ways. Rehearse all that you have learned and understand about facing challenges. Make the interpretation of hard times a standard part of your leadership growth training strategy.

Don't ignore the pain and difficulty caused by opposing forces.

To battle through the tough times, we must name our pain and own the consequences of it. Honest conversation and debate within your team usually turns out to be extremely important and worthwhile as you move through times of darkness and difficulty. This is simply what teams do.

Stick together when the times are tough; you'll create a new context for amazing progress once you pass through your rough patch.

Teams who have been through the fire together tend to be strengthened in resolve, knowledge, commitment, and wisdom. Teams that fragment in the tough times seldom come back together on the other end of the tunnel. Regarding tough times as opportunities for growth, change, and renewed engagement usually means that such times can, and often will, be exactly that.

Make time for evaluating your challenges, to the end that you craft effective strategies for making a way through the hard times.

People need space to process tough times. We do no one a favor by capping conversation. Finding ways to talk through challenges and to build reflective time into your own life and the culture of your team will be essential to turning setbacks and hard times into inspiring examples of success and surprising wins. Making space for individual evaluation, soul-searching, and even "alone time" will pay off for your team.

Make sure that you aren't the primary source of your own challenges.

While difficulty can be expected as normal for anyone or any group engaged in a mission of significance, we must remain alert to our own responsibility in inviting hard times due to a lack of diligence, inattention to detail, a want of commitment to excellence, personal failure, or simple selfishness. As leaders, we must make honesty our operative value as we reflect here. Invite others into the evaluative process. I have experienced blind spots in my own life and work that prevent me from seeing important aspects of my own complicity in creating undue conflict, challenge, and obstacles. Identifying the blind spots with the help of trusted teammates will go a long way to making your team stronger and your work more trusted both within and outside your organization. In such circumstances, I've learned, often the hard way, the real benefit of admitting mistakes, making amends, and simply apologizing. Admitting failure (see Chapter One) only adds to your credibility as a leader.

Your Turn

1. Think about a time when you struggled against opposition or darkness. What did you need most in the midst of that experience? Why? How did the experience make you feel? Did you come out of it feeling positive or negative? Why?

2. Now recall a time when a team you were a part of or were leading faced opposition. How did you react to the struggle? What did your team need from you? If you were a leader at the time, how did you feel? What did you do? Were you satisfied with the outcome? What did you learn? What could you have done differently or better?

3. Do you believe struggle and opposition can be a good thing? Why or why not?

4. When you feel afraid, how do you respond? Explain.

5. As a leader, when you've felt like you were in a dark tunnel, what did you do? Spend a few moments reflecting on that experience. What did you learn? How did you resolve the situation? Or did you? How did your team react to the struggle, as well as to your handling of it?

6. The next time you find yourself in a struggle, what, if anything, will you do differently?

NOTE

[1] David Halberstam, *The Children* (New York: Random House, 1998).

CHAPTER THREE

HONOR TRADITION; CELEBRATE INNOVATION

Loving the past, along with all its passions and the very values that created and shaped us, is a natural and an essential part of being human. At the same time, appreciating heritage gives us the freedom, the confidence, and the joy necessary to modify and innovate as we move forward into the challenges of a new, unknown world. That said, in a constantly evolving world of discovery as complex and expansive as ours, we must learn to adapt. We must investigate new options. We understand life and calling as a process, a journey, a movement. As a result, change becomes a prerequisite for progress. In the words of Anthony de Mello, "The one who would be constant in happiness must frequently change."[1] Substitute "success" or "effectiveness" for de Mello's "happiness" and you get my drift.

Nothing of significance involving improving the quality of life is ever settled. We must be willing to investigate the benefits and possibilities afforded us by change. Standing on the shoulders of those who passed before us and building on their learnings and legacies, we must be open to continuing the journey—but always on our own terms and in direct response to every new context or circumstance. Most of the time, we would be well advised to hold tradition and innovation in a creative, dynamic tension.

I appreciate the insights Texas Rangers Baseball Club hitting coach Anthony Iapoce expressed about the team's 2016 players Adrián Beltré and Carlos Beltrán: "What keeps them going is they'll tell you they don't have it figured out, which is what great people do in any profession. They'll never say they have it figured out."[2] Assuming that things can improve, that there is likely a better, more effective way to play the game, keeps healthy people and organizations moving forward. Effective leaders assume that "increasing impact" is included in their job descriptions, no matter where they stack up in the organization's chart of team members and responsibilities.

A commitment to trying to "figure it out" is what I look for in anyone I interview for a spot at CitySquare. A passion for pursuing excellence always includes an enthusiastic determination to embrace change for the better. Every mission can be accomplished more effectively. When inspired by deepening devotion to your mission, every decision to change things will be worth the difficulty and the effort. Of course, a major challenge will involve bringing everyone along with you and your new, ever-evolving vision.

Change as Progress

The wonderful people who founded the organization where I work intended to establish a center of relief, hope, and betterment for low-income individuals and families living in inner city East Dallas. Through the early years, scores of volunteers assisted thousands of their neighbors with food, rental and utility assistance, medical and dental services, and employment readiness training. The entire enterprise emerged from the religious faith of the founders, as well as the many volunteers involved. While we do things very differently today compared to the beginning, we continue to acknowledge the great, loving contributions these pioneers made as they began. We wouldn't be here today without their contributions and the strong tradition upon which they built.

Still, learning takes place. Evaluations lead to discoveries. Policies change, as do methods. If our focus is on our "customers," we will be concerned with adapting constantly for their benefit, and not our own. And, across the years, we've done just that. At times, especially in the early days of change and innovation, tension arose as people considered our changes and our ways of operating as too "newfangled"!

Increasingly, our mission trained our eyes and hearts on the neighbors who approached us seeking help and some measure of hope, respect, and purpose.

As a result, we changed.

We invited our customers to join us as volunteers.

We blurred the lines that separated the so-called "poor" from our team of mostly so-called "rich."

Our volunteer base expanded wildly as we made the changes. The growth in the number of volunteers available to us proved dramatic. We decided to harness the people power that presented itself to us. We innovated—and with marked success. The story is much longer[3]—in fact, it continues today! We remain dedicated to pursuing innovative approaches to our work with our inner city neighbors who've become our friends and partners.

Change as Disruption

However, we were disruptive—in some cases extremely disruptive. Not everyone stayed with us. Some of the earliest volunteers resigned in frustration. Some left feeling displaced and no longer needed. I'm sure we could have done a better job of attempting to integrate them into the new systems we were hard at work building. Possibly, we were impatient. Maybe we exhibited arrogance. I am sure we failed in many cases. I know for sure that I failed again and again in ushering in a different approach as we sought to be more effective in working *with* our neighbors rather than *for* them.

But we tried. We really did.

We trained.

We pleaded.

We exhibited.

We experimented.

We explained.

We taught.

We counseled and consoled.

At the end of that early day, we certainly changed the conversation—and almost overnight.

And, over the course of time, we established a new culture of innovation.

We honored the values of our founders: generosity, respect, love, stewardship, compassion, and charity. We just found new ways to express those values. We translated the same values in words and actions that made more "connective sense" to our community.

Innovation and Disruption: Housing First

Innovation (and even the suggestion of innovative change) most always leads to disruption to one degree or another. Tradition feels more reliable in terms of outcomes and identity. Most of the time, we discover a satisfying firmness in the reliability of tradition and its long-cherished process and recognized culture. Most of us like to think of ourselves as innovators. That is, until the storms of change break overhead! "We've always done it this way" can sound mighty good when someone suggests some wild-eyed new approach chocked full of risk!

One of the most disruptive and successful social sector innovations of the last quarter century is the Housing First movement. That's correct: Housing First has become a social movement. Devotees can sound like evangelists promoting a newly discovered religion! At times, purists border on obnoxious. But Housing First works, and there's big data to make that case.

About two decades ago, the father of Housing First, Sam Tsemberis, discovered and began to gather data that revealed the inadequacies of traditional approaches to addressing homelessness in the United States.[4] In short, Tsemberis discovered that no verifiable, statistical advantage in terms of housing stability and resident well-being can be found in housing programs that erect barriers making housing hard to enter for those experiencing homelessness. Requiring perfect sobriety in order to maintain housing and punishing people who "fall off the wagon" of their recovery programs results in no better outcomes than simply placing a person in permanent housing before working on various recovery issues, even when a person fails.

Housing First defines an extremely simple strategy for housing homeless persons. What is the solution to homelessness? A home. It is about that straightforward. Placing a person into permanent housing and making available the choice of supportive services works better at interrupting the homeless cycle than other approaches or methodologies. It just works if you follow the pathway that has been proven effective over the past twenty-five years or so. Here's how it works.

First, locate a person in need of housing. Sources here include emergency shelters, outdoor encampments, transitional housing programs, other "housing ready" initiatives, sidewalks, faith communities in touch with homeless people, jails, hospital discharge stations, mental health facilities, and community-based health centers. Wherever people live without permanent housing, there you will find perfect candidates for a Housing First program.

Second, locate a housing unit. Possible sources here include all of a community's vacant housing stock: single-family houses, multifamily duplexes and apartments, tiny houses, single-resident occupancy units, studio apartments, lofts, and flats, to mention a few.[5] In short, a qualifying unit is one designed and fit for human habitation.

Third, find a funding source for occupant rents. This is a simple business fact: in any project taken to scale, someone must pay rent on the housing units one way or the other if the project is to be sustainable. Examples of payer sources include federally funded housing choice vouchers, project-based housing vouchers, and public housing development units. Project-based housing vouchers prove to be an attractive source of housing payments for developers of housing for the homeless. Vouchers of this type link rental payment to a specific housing unit in a specified development to which the voucher remains attached even if the resident leaves for other housing options. This approach to funding rents provides stability to the development for a contracted term regardless of the tenants who may come and go. Other possible payer sources include charitable organizations' housing units, as well as units funded by local Continuum of Care groups that access and utilize funding directly from the U.S. Department of Housing and Urban Development (HUD).

Fourth, place the person in housing with virtually no strings attached. In our housing program at CitySquare, we have one basic rule: be a good neighbor. Failure in maintaining sobriety doesn't automatically mean a person loses her apartment. The genius of Housing First is that housing can be maintained while a person continues to work on personal, life-robbing issues.

Still battling drugs or alcohol? Keep your struggle out of the common areas of the larger housing development and you will maintain your housing. Bring your struggles into the common areas, then we need to have a serious, direct talk about your future as a participant in the housing program.

Often, I tell people if I drink a half bottle of Scotch whiskey some night but keep that stupid experience inside my house, the only force of nature I will face and have to deal with is my wife! However, as soon as I bring that same experience into my front yard or onto my street, then I've got the entire neighborhood to deal with, including the police most likely.

Housing First allows people to work on their problems and life goals from the stable platform of secure housing. A fundamental part of the process involves the free formation of community, often the budding of new relationships, and adoption of completely new categories of service philosophy. The resident remains in charge of his life, his plans, and his future. The option to choose or to reject the available wraparound services always remains with the tenant. As people enter the Housing First housing units offered by CitySquare, we share with them a vision for a strong, vibrant community in which they will be invited to play a major role. Respect remains the primary value in every part of the path into housing. Respect continues for the resident, regardless of the choices he makes about participation in our program offerings.

Our concierge[6] team works hard to build trust while conveying information about the myriad opportunities for growth and expanded horizons. As trust grows, residents begin to imagine again a future complete with goals, objectives, and aspirations. Our team works alongside residents to assist in whatever way possible to see those dreams realized. You name it—transportation to a doctor's appointment, help filling a prescription, connection to a skills class, a timely trip to the grocery store across town, even tickets to the opera!

Our team tries to be present in the fulfillment of dreams for people who've not dreamed in a long, long time.

Thanks to the analysis and the data gathered by practitioners like Tsemberis, and to the successful results of those employing the clear innovation, Housing First now defines the priorities and the requirements for funding community-based housing programs by HUD. But these changes have been extremely disruptive in my community.

Members of the local Continuum of Care, the local community group required by HUD for communities to receive funding for housing, resisted changing to a Housing First model, at least in the beginning. Change became more typical after our community lost over one million dollars in funding due to our low scores against HUD requirements regarding Housing First as the primary approach for housing programs that the agency would approve and fund.

And, frankly, in a "churched up" community like Dallas, Texas, the broad freedom allowed to tenants by the Housing First philosophy didn't mesh well with "housing readiness" programs, especially those requiring complete sobriety before entering housing.

However, the disruption sparked by the development of Housing First projects has been a positive development. The disruption birthed deeper conversations and systems change across the board in our city, and the same has been the case across the nation.

Again, consider the logic of how we usually regard a homeless alcoholic. Many housing programs require an alcoholic to maintain complete sobriety for an extended period of time before she is judged housing-ready. As I consider how hard it is to master any deep-seated life challenge such as alcoholism without a real home—not just shelter, but a place of my own with a front door I can lock, a bathroom all to myself, and a wall where I can hang a picture—it hits me that we impose harsher standards on the poorest and weakest people among us than on the rest of us who enjoy all the security we need.

Think about it for a moment. What percentage of the population of alcoholics in the United States enjoys the benefit of permanent housing? I'd put that number at well over 90 percent. Alcoholics run companies, teach school, serve as police officers, provide pastoral leadership to faith communities, fly airplanes, and engineer the building of cities. Still, the vast majority of this group is housed.

Yet our traditional approach to the homeless alcoholic has been to deny the one thing that might provide a stable platform for working successfully on recovery: a home. Why would we impose such a harsh standard upon the homeless poor while giving the housed a break, even though many deal with the same personal life problems? The disruption of innovation leads to real progress grounded in new questions like this one.

Innovation and tradition battle it out in most organizations. Tradition feels more reliable, especially in times of change and instability, but at the price of organizational stagnation. Innovation offers new effectiveness, but only to the extent of an organization's capacity to live with a measure of risk. Everything seems to come down to a risk-reward equation. These days, we cannot avoid risk if we expect to get results. And the added benefit delivered via the creativity sparked by disruption almost always makes the risk worth it and necessary.

Your Turn

1. On a scale of 1 to 10, with one being "Incurable Traditionalist" and ten being "Enthusiastic Innovator," where do you land? Explain.

2. Describe a time when you faced a situation calling for a new approach. How did you react? How did you feel as you worked in that experience? What did you learn about yourself? Your team? What was the result?

3. In a world of constant and quickening change, how do you lead others? How do you prepare yourself for your challenging context?

4. Based on what you've read here, does Housing First appeal to you? Explain.

5. If you are a traditionalist at heart, how do you respond to innovators on your team? How do they make you feel? Share an experience.

6. If you are an innovator, how do you respond to traditionalists on your team? How do they make you feel? Share an experience.

7. Can innovation be taught like a skill? Explain.

NOTES

[1]Anthony de Mello, *Awareness: The Perils and Opportunities of Reality* (New York: Image Books, 1990), Kindle.

[2]Tyler Kepner, "Baseball's Grand Old Men, Like the Rangers, Still Seek First Ring," *New York Times*, September 14, 2016, https://www.nytimes.com/2016/09/15/sports/baseball/adrian-beltre-carlos-beltran-texas-rangers.html.

[3]Read much more about CitySquare's story of change and our commitment to innovation in the social justice sector in my book *The Wealth of the Poor: How Valuing Every Neighbor Restores Hope in Our Cities* (Abilene Christian University Press, 2013).

[4]To learn more about the expansive world of Tsemberis and Housing First, visit http://www.pathwayshousingfirst.org/.

[5]Of course, we might not expect to discover many viable, qualifying units in every part of a community. And this is one of the big challenges to developing scattered site housing units that include upscale areas. The federal courts continue to debate the issue of housing discrimination and deepening segregation as they consider the legitimate uses of public funds to provide housing for all, including "high opportunity" neighborhoods. To read more on the 2015 U.S. Supreme Court decision on housing discrimination in Dallas, Texas, see: http://www.npr.org/sections/thetwo-way/2015/06/25/417433460 /in-fair-housing-act-case-supreme-court-backs-disparate-impact-claims. The decision was muddled a year later by a Fifth Circuit Court of Appeals ruling: http://www.tml.org/legis_updates/legis_update111810h_fairhousing.

[6]Words matter. People probably tire of hearing me use the word "concierge" in reference to our Neighbor Support Services team of case managers, but words matter. We are attempting to convey a new way of doing business among and alongside the poorest people among us. So humor me!

CHAPTER FOUR

DON'T DISMISS
THE DIFFICULT

Ease of accomplishment too often eliminates or cuts against the grain of the artistic, the revolutionary, and the stupendous. Many times, real solutions to the problems we face turn out to be downright difficult. Working through difficulties to achieve a worthy objective results in invaluable credibility for organizations and leaders, credibility that can be utilized in future projects and in unimagined ways.

At the same time, when we attack difficult issues, we can face opposition in the form of critics who demean our best efforts, constituents who question our judgment, and competitors who choose an easier way. Try something monumental and prepare for the trolls who are quick to criticize! Still, refusing to address difficult challenges, when given the opportunity, usually results in outcomes that set back communities. Turning away from the difficulties of life stunts the growth and advancement of individuals. Over the years, I've learned to pay attention when someone declares, "It is just too hard to do." The "too difficult" argument causes my ears to perk up and my adrenalin to rush. Nothing changes without the willingness of engaged people to tackle what presents and appears as an impossible job. It's true that the shortest distance between two points is a straight line. However, what's true in geometry may not work best in daily life where the way to real quality can be exasperating and beyond circuitous!

Doing What's Right Can Be Difficult: A Transformative Story

Tackling difficult problems can be forced on us by our values. At times of intense difficulty, we discover who we really are and what we intend to become. This is true for both individuals and groups. If our values don't lead us to respond to difficulty with vigor, hope, hard work, and risk, we may need to reconsider either our values or our commitment to them and to our mission.

While serving a church in Richardson, Texas, a suburban community in North Dallas County, I developed an important friendship with a dedicated physician, Dr. Kevin Murray. Early in 1985, Murray called me with an unusual question. He had begun treating a growing group of patients who tested positive for a strange new virus that would soon fill the news. Human immunodeficiency virus (HIV), when full-blown, destroys the immune system of those it attacks. Acquired immunodeficiency syndrome (AIDS), still a mystery at the time, amounted to a death sentence for a number of Murray's patients. During that first phone conversation, he asked me if I could meet with one of his patients whose disease had progressed to end-stage AIDS. He informed me that the young man, not yet thirty years old, had grown up in a fundamentalist religious tradition, but felt he could not go there for spiritual comfort due to his disease and his homosexuality. He needed a minister. The question was, would I meet with him? I agreed to a meeting, not knowing what to expect.

"Steve" represented my first personal encounter with AIDS. A pleasant young man and a fourth-year student at Baylor College of Dentistry, he got right to the point. He explained his faith background, which I understood all too well. And then, he asked the question he had come to ask. "Larry, do you think we can become well enough acquainted so that you can perform my funeral?"

His honesty and his need stunned me.

Of course, I agreed.

After he left my office, I had to deal with my own emotions, not the least of which was fear. At the time, I didn't understand much about this new, deadly disease. I can remember going to the restroom and scrubbing my hands for a long time—a good routine, but an ill-informed response to my new friend's tragic personal dilemma. A better reaction was my commitment to learn all that I could about his condition. Over the next several months, we developed a friendship. Authentic, but also rushed and born of terrible necessity, our relationship drew me into the difficult world of HIV/AIDS. I was with "Steve" the night that he died. And, as he requested, I presided at his memorial service. Tragically, the faith tradition of this man's family had no word of comfort or compassion to offer.

Thanks to Dr. Murray, "Steve" stood at the front of a long line of men and women who entered my world and the life of the church over the next several years. To prepare the congregation for what I knew was ahead of us, we rolled out a comprehensive plan to educate and inform about the quickly approaching community challenge and our planned response. Midweek study sessions with leaders, Sunday evening training classes and consultations for several weeks, and, finally, two Sunday morning sermons combined to get HIV/AIDS on the radar screen of the entire church.

As the information spread and as it became clear that the church would respond with compassion and practical, helpful service to those who came to us with the awful malady, a handful of members expressed concern and fear: What if the disease spread much more easily than we were being told? What if it was airborne? What if it mutated to become wildly communicable?

We did our best to address every question. We lined up health experts to speak to the church and its various groups. At the end of the day, we communicated that if the disease were to be as easy to acquire as some radio reactionaries suggested, we were all doomed anyway and that the best way through the supposed coming crisis was to live and die in service to others. The critics seemed to recede, at least in their vocal dissent.

As word spread that our church welcomed persons with HIV/AIDS, more victims and families showed up. In addition, as we reached out to other community groups committed to responding to the special needs of these people, we began receiving more and more referrals involving people who were dealing with the health crisis in isolation and without spiritual resources.

My friend and partner in HIV/AIDS ministry, Rev. Scott Allen, called one day to tell me about the case of Lynn Stanfield. Scott worked with the Christian Life Commission inside the Baptist General Convention of Texas. Lynn's situation illustrated the response of most churches to the escalating crisis. Lynn contracted the virus from an infected sexual partner a couple of years prior to her marriage to her husband, James. She discovered that she was HIV positive on Christmas Eve the year before we met. The couple's young son also tested HIV positive.

Lynn was shocked and devastated by the harsh facts of her reality. James had a history of drug abuse but was making progress with his sobriety and had responded with strong support when Lynn learned of her condition. The Stanfields found a small Southern Baptist church in Richardson that they began attending on a regular basis. James had been attracted to the church's pastor, an older man who provided a kind of support that proved very beneficial to him.

The couple decided to join the church, but on leaving a Sunday morning service, Lynn asked the pastor to drop by so that they could visit. Lynn wanted the minister and the church to understand her situation and her illness completely. When the pastor called to make an appointment to visit, Lynn decided to tell him her situation. When she informed him that she had tested positive for HIV, a long silence ensued on the phone line. After a bit more conversation, the pastor informed Lynn that she and James and their family should look for another church.

Learning of the situation from Scott Allen, I called and set up a time to visit with the couple. I let them know that they would be welcome at our church and that we were prepared to assist in whatever way we could. Ironically, the first Sunday morning that the Stanfields visited Richardson East, I delivered the first of my two-part series on AIDS. In that message, I talked about the nature of the disease and the cause and the prognosis of its course in a human life. I also laid out our church's commitment to stand with and among those who suffered its devastating effects. I challenged the church to begin taking advantage of the training and additional information that would be forthcoming in our programming and education plans.

At the end of that service, Lynn Stanfield walked down the aisle to join the church. As we talked at the front of the sanctuary, she told me that she wanted me to tell the church about her illness and her family. I informed her that such a disclosure was not a requirement for membership in the church. She assured me that she felt it absolutely necessary for everyone to understand what she and her family faced. James accompanied her but told me that he wasn't prepared to join the church on that first morning. Given his experience with churches, he felt a need to get more familiar with us.

When I turned to address the congregation, I introduced Lynn and told the church that she had HIV/AIDS. I shared as much detail of her story as I could in my short "welcome to the church" greeting. Then, during the closing hymn and benediction, I must confess that I held my breath to see how the congregation would respond.

To my delight, people stood in line for over forty-five minutes to welcome Lynn and her family. And people were honest, as well as affirming and welcoming. I recall one dear lady who stood at arm's length from Lynn and told her, "I'm sorry, I can't hug you today. But one day soon, I know I will be able to. We are glad you are here."

Others dove right in to a friendship with Lynn and her family. Her life mobilized amazing action and engagement on the part of the church. She taught us a great deal. Her circumstances pressed upon us the importance of putting faith and compassion to work, as well as the realization that when that occurred, real change transpired for everyone.

Lynn was an amazing person. As we did more and more to educate the church and the community about the nature of HIV and its spread, on more than one occasion Lynn got up from her bed, even when she felt terrible, to participate in panel discussions and to give her testimony regarding HIV/AIDS and to discuss how people of faith and humanity could and should respond.

Lynn's death touched thousands of people, just as her life transformed countless others, including so many in our church. *D Magazine* published a cover feature story on her struggle and her life.[1] Our church was featured in that report, but we all recognized that Lynn was the real story and the true hero.

"John's" story remains in my heart. A fifty-five-year-old gay man, John came to our church by referral from his doctor. When he first began attending our gatherings, he sat quietly at the rear of the auditorium, usually among a group of older members of the church. In their typical fashion, this wonderful group of "old timers," as they referred to themselves, befriended him and made him feel welcome. After several months, he joined the church. Raised in a very conservative church in another part of Texas, John found a great deal of peace in our midst. His family included a brother who was an elder in the family church back at home. He also had two grown sons who were in college. He had hidden and attempted to deal with his homosexuality for all his adult life, coming out after his sons were grown and gone from home. John's partner began attending the church as well. Both men were HIV positive and both moved into full-blown AIDS shortly after coming to our congregation. John died after about two years of difficult struggle. His funeral service and burial took place in his hometown. Before the funeral service, his brother called me to ask if we could host a memorial service after the burial so that the church and John's friends in Dallas might gather to honor his memory and at the same time provide his family an opportunity to thank everyone for their kindness to John during his ordeal. We gladly agreed.

The memorial service took place on a Monday evening at the church. Several hundred people gathered to honor and remember John. It was a remarkable night in so many ways. The most amazing thing about the entire evening was the audience makeup and the response of the church members to our guests. About half of the crowd was from the church, with most of that group composed of our older members who had formed close ties to John. They sat on one side of the sanctuary. The other half of the audience, seated on the other side of the room, was made up of John's friends, mostly from the gay and lesbian community in Dallas. After the service ended, I watched as our older members crossed the center aisle to welcome John's friends. The manner in which our members welcomed these special guests and the way in which both groups engaged one another moved me to tears.

Working with men, women, and children living with HIV/AIDS presented unique, difficult, and trying challenges. As a result, we were always on the lookout for new resources to assist in the process. As mentioned already, I met Scott Allen while learning how best to serve and relate to the growing numbers of people who came to us seeking solace and peace as their lives and the lives of those they loved ebbed away. Scott's work with the Christian Life Commission resulted in the production of extremely useful pastoral resources for those who worked in this space. I called Scott once after receiving a helpful collection of materials assembled in a handy file folder clearly marked as "AIDS Resource for Pastors." I'll never forget our phone conversation.

"Scott, I just received the file folder of pastoral resources on the AIDS crisis. It is so well done and extremely helpful, possibly the best resources that I have seen," I told him.

"Well thanks, Larry. We hoped it would be useful," he responded. "I appreciate your call and your encouragement."

"No problem, Scott. I have to say that the piece in the packet entitled 'A Mother's Story' is powerful beyond words. I just had to call and commend you for your work on this particular educational tool," I went on.

The essay I had in mind told the tragic story of a mother who contracted the virus during a blood transfusion while she was pregnant with her first child, but didn't discover the problem until she became pregnant with her second child a few years later. Here was a case of a married woman and a mother of two small children facing certain death within a few years given the state of medical technology at the time. In addition, both of her children were found to be HIV positive. Only the father had escaped the heinous virus.

After my comment, there was a long pause on the other end of the call.

"Larry, you know that story is the story of my wife, Lydia, and our children, Bryan and Matt, don't you?" Scott informed me grimly.

"No!" I exclaimed. "I had no idea, Scott. I am so sorry."

Scott spent the next half hour telling me their story, a story even more disheartening and unjust than what the single page had conveyed.[2] Scott had been a Southern Baptist minister. In fact, he was the son of a renowned Baptist preacher, Jimmy Allen. In the late 1970s, the elder Allen had been president of the Southern Baptist Convention and had served as the president of the Southern Baptist Radio and Television Commission in charge of all the denomination's media productions. From 1960 to 1968, the senior Allen served as executive secretary of the Texas Christian Life Commission. Much of his work during this period involved his preaching a strong, anti-racism message to the churches in his charge, not a popular message among many Texas Baptists at the time. While serving with the giant First Baptist Church of San Antonio, Allen led his wealthy downtown church in developing an array of outreach efforts to the poor and the homeless. Allen was also a close friend of President Jimmy Carter and an effective leader and thinker among progressive Baptists.

In 1982, Scott and Lydia had been living in San Francisco while Scott served as pastor to a small Southern Baptist church in Pacifica, California, and completed his seminary education at Golden Gate Baptist Theological Seminary. Their first child, Matthew, had been born while they were there, and it was on the night before his birth that Lydia had received the tainted blood transfusion without knowing of its effect. Matthew's arrival was accompanied with serious complications and the infant underwent intestinal surgery shortly after his birth. Over the next three years, Matthew and his mother were not well. Matthew didn't grow as he should have and battled persistent ear infections. Lydia experienced infections, colds, night sweats, and shingles.

After graduation the same year Matthew was born, the Allens moved to Colorado Springs, Colorado, where Scott took a position with First Christian Church (Disciples of Christ) as an associate minister. In May 1985, Lydia gave birth to the couple's second child, Bryan. Born prematurely and with heart defects, the child struggled from the beginning of his life. In September 1985, the Allens learned the truth about the illness afflicting Lydia and her sons. The San Francisco blood bank called to report that the transfusion Lydia had received prior to Matt's birth might have been contaminated with HIV. Tests confirmed that Lydia, Matthew, and Bryan were HIV positive. Only Scott tested negative.

After receiving the crushing report, Scott informed the senior minister at the church where he served of his family's situation. The minister responded by demanding Scott's resignation by the next morning. Scott told me how he and Lydia left the city "under the cover of dark." The Allens moved to Fort Worth, Texas, where he had many contacts in the church world, especially among the Southern Baptists. Sadly, the Allens could find no church that was prepared to receive the family as members. About this time, Scott went to work for the Christian Life Commission. His area of focus, not surprisingly, was HIV/AIDS. I found his story difficult to absorb. My emotions included anger and deep despair.

"Scott, you and your family can certainly come to Richardson East. We'd be honored to have you with us!" I told him what he likely already knew. "You would be most welcome, and you would be a huge asset to us."

"I know, Larry, and thanks for the invitation," he responded. "But, you know, it's just too late for us. We've basically given up on church."

Indeed, by then, Scott looked to Eastern religions in his quest for understanding and spirituality. For him, Christians had offered too little, too late, and they had no ultimate answers in the face of the enormous pain he had endured.

Unknown to me, by the time I met Scott and Lydia Allen, their youngest son, Bryan, had passed away. Little Bryan died in January 1986, the first known infant in Dallas County to die of congenital AIDS. Following his death, Lydia had thrown herself into the development of a pediatric housing service for children with AIDS. The result was Bryan's House, established and named in her youngest son's honor and memory. The facility led the way in Dallas via its stellar record in caring for children and families who dealt with the deadly syndrome.

The blows to Scott and his family continued to be severe. Lydia died on February 28, 1992.

The summer prior to Matt's first grade year, I noticed a story in the *Dallas Morning News* decrying the dearth of childcare available to families whose little ones had HIV/AIDS, especially in the summer months. As I read the article with interest, it hit me that the reporter was describing Matt Allen's situation for the approaching summer. I made a few phone calls to confirm my suspicion. My hunch turned out to be correct. I spoke to Scott and told him that we intended to open our full-service childcare center to children with HIV/AIDS.

Scott thanked me but warned me that we needed to be careful and that he didn't expect we could pull it off. He feared that once other parents knew of the presence of an infected child, they would withdraw their children and our center would be ruined. I listened to his counsel but asked him to give me a couple of weeks to work on it.

The next two to three weeks felt like a whirlwind of difficult activity. After receiving preliminary approval from the church board to proceed with a short study, investigation, and community education plan, we all went to work. We consulted with the physicians who were members of the church, and we listened to the advice of other medical professionals whom they brought in for us. We organized a childcare center parents' meeting. At the meeting, we informed the parents that we intended to begin receiving children with HIV/AIDS into the center. We let them know that we would not identify who the children were, but on our "illness warning" board, HIV/AIDS would be permanently listed for all to see. At that meeting, medical professionals answered questions and encouraged the parents not to panic and that there would be no reason to withdraw their children. We asked parents to call us for private consultation, and we made ourselves available to any who desired a conference.

Thanks to the cooperation of our leaders, the unity of our staff, and the openness of the parents, we only lost a single child due to the policy change because we lost one staff person whose child used the childcare services. The child's father insisted that his wife resign and their child be withdrawn from both the center and the church.

Matthew Allen was a special little boy. As a preschooler, Matt knew more about HIV/AIDS than most adults. The real dangers involved in Matt using our childcare services were all his dangers. A simple cold or other infection could have ended his life. In the case of a cut or an injury that might include the loss of blood, Matt knew exactly what to do to ensure the safety of everyone around him. He was a bright, caring, kind, wonderful little boy.

In 1995, Matt died at age twelve while in the seventh grade here in Dallas.

When the national media learned of the story of the Allen family, they began calling for our input. The irony of the reaction of churches to this family with a record of multi-generational, life-long service escaped no one's attention.

Among the calls I received was one from the producer of NBC's *Dateline* news program. Not long after that first call, Jane Pauley made a trip to Dallas and set up a broadcast set in our sanctuary for an interview with me about our seemingly unique response to the Allen family and their situation. Pauley also toured our childcare center and spoke to our staff and to parents about their take on the issue. It was an exciting and sobering morning, and a great opportunity to spread the truth about HIV/AIDS and how local congregations could get involved to make things a bit more bearable for those affected.

Creating a "Difficulty Inventory"

As I've thought more intentionally about facing difficult challenges, I've discovered a helpful exercise. Begin by thinking back over a period in your life or career or marriage or you fill in the blank. Next, simply list the major difficult challenges you decided to address. In each case, use just a few words to describe major obstacles, those things that made it difficult. Then, note any clear outcomes. Something like this:

Project/Circumstance	Difficulty	Outcome
Cottages at Hickory Crossing	Funding/length of construction	fifty homes for homeless
Public contracts	Administrative challenges	Funding to scale key projects
Coaching inner city youth baseball players	Inexperienced coach lack of resources	Kids learned teamwork/skills

● ● ● ● ● ◯ ● ● ● ● ●

One of the obvious benefits of this exercise is that it allows you to compare the difficult challenge to the resulting clear benefits of the effort applied against the challenge. Taking stock of accomplishment in the face of difficult circumstances and opportunities motivates me to work even harder and to never, never give up just because a challenge turns out to be difficult.

One note of caution: attempting to take on too many challenging, difficult assignments at once can be hazardous to your health and the health of your team. Some people can handle numerous difficult assignments at once, but everyone has their limits. What is true for an individual is also true for a team of people. Staying in touch by keeping the lines of communication open will be essential here, both for individuals and groups. Being able to consult and debrief with leaders and team members is essential in the process of facing, overcoming, and solving difficult challenges. Each person or team member must honestly assess capacity.

Not long ago, our team faced a challenging offer from the State of Texas. Dallas County needed to find a single partner to administer the state's Community Service Block Grant funds. Interestingly, we applied for this role with the state about fifteen years earlier, but we did not win the grant contract competition at that time. When the new opportunity crossed my desk, I was excited! In fact, we had known for several months that the fund would open up to us and to other nonprofit groups in the county. My enthusiasm needed to be tempered because the fund carried with it several difficult requirements that would affect our board structure, dictate to some extent the number of locations we would be required to develop and manage, and impose relatively onerous reporting requirements. After several days of careful and critical analysis, the team voted not to pursue the opportunity. I was disappointed, but it was voted down overwhelmingly. Our process and due diligence resulted in the right decision for our entire team.

Leaders must learn to acquiesce to their teams. Being voted down and embracing such action builds a team's heart and soul. Everyone on the team worked extra hard not to disappoint me. But the team knew better than the boss!

Curiously, several weeks after we informed the city and the state of our decision not to apply for the funding, the city invited us to join a new collaboration of organizations. As part of a larger team, we will be able to contribute to the community effort while remaining true to our mission and purpose. By turning down the earlier option when it wasn't a fit for us, we found ourselves in position to do our work on our terms and within our capacity. In this scenario, everyone will win.

Your Turn

1. What did you learn from the stories in this chapter? What, if anything, made you feel uncomfortable? What made sense? What if this church group had done nothing?
2. Consider how you respond when faced with difficulty. Plot your normal response on the scale below.

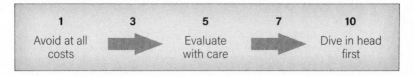

1	3	5	7	10
Avoid at all costs		Evaluate with care		Dive in head first

3. Describe a difficult challenge you've faced. How did you react? How did you feel as you worked through the challenge? What did you learn about yourself and your team? What was the result?
4. How do you lead your team through hard times? Provide an example.

5. Do you agree that leaders must not shy away from the
   difficult?
6. How helpful is the idea of a "difficulty inventory"?

NOTES

[1]Lynn was provided the pseudonym "Ann Ellison" to protect her identity
and that of her family in "AIDS: Seven Days in the Crisis," Skip Hollingsworth,
D Magazine, March 1988, pp. 46ff. See also "Editor's Page: The politics of AIDS:
a bitter struggle for compassion and money," 6.

[2]Jimmy Allen, *Burden of a Secret: A Story of Truth and Mercy in the Face of
AIDS* (Moorings, NY: Random House, 1995).

CHAPTER FIVE

FORGET THE CREDITS

I suppose it's simply human nature. We work hard, at times remarkably hard! We, and significant others in our lives, sacrifice. We pay the price necessary to accomplish our work. We feel good about our accomplishments. We realize at the deepest place in our souls that our work matters; it is important and results in satisfying outcomes. We even receive praise, appreciation, and affirmation as a result of our endeavors. If we are honest about it, the recognition provides genuine satisfaction. It just feels good to be given the credit for work well done, whatever the field, project, or focus.

Taking credit for success seems logical, but only if we are satisfied with small thinking.

Moving beyond Small Thinking

Insisting on taking credit for the work we do and for the accomplishments we enjoy represents a small, even narrow, limited approach to life. In fact, almost every significant achievement is the result of a team of people who conspire, coordinate, and cooperate to accomplish what so often someone else has imagined, planned, and underwritten.

When I take stock honestly and consider the actual fabric of my life story, this truth comes into sharp focus for me. Every advantage I enjoy today is the result of the work, forethought, and investment of a large number of other people. My parents, my wife, my children, my grandchildren, my friends, my teachers, my mentors, my ministers, the people with whom and for whom I work and have worked all my life, even strangers and circumstances encountered along the way—so many people, in so many ways, with so many assets and options have shared life and opportunity with me that there is never a time I can honestly take exclusive credit for whatever success may result from my life or efforts.

Add into this life equation my position of unbelievable privilege when compared to the majority of people on the earth, and you have the rationale for a life that insists on living in a much larger way. By an accident of birth, I possess power, countless options, doors of opportunity that swing open for me whenever I approach them, and unfair advantages over others who don't share my gender, my race, my educational background, or my inherent privilege. Given the backdrop of my life, I have no reason to take any credit before I give most of it away to those who populate my past, my present, and certainly my future.

Sure, I'm successful by many standards. But that is not the point. With all my advantage, shame on me if I don't get things done! And then, the reality remains: I don't always get things done!

What I'm mainly talking about here is attitude.

It's all about a life perspective.

If life is a baseball game, I was born on third base. If I don't score, I can only blame myself. If I do cross the plate, I'm eager to pass the credit along to countless other people who deserve more credit than I for my success.

To live a larger life, it is extremely important to get this part right. People who face and fully appreciate their privilege and advantages in life will find it natural and, eventually, even essential to redirect the credit to others when it starts to come their way. Getting the "credit-advantage-expectation" formula right turns out to be an important step in getting important things done. People who don't master this special form of "social mathematics" seldom think large enough to address and solve the problems we can expect to face in our increasingly close and complex world. Leaders, especially, who react instinctively to experiences of success and breakthrough accomplishments by passing along credit and congratulations will be wildly successful in building confident, resilient teams. Leaders who master the fine art of passing along credit will have no problems in attracting and retaining essential talent.

Tobias Fredberg studied the leadership habits of top executives in thirty-six companies when it comes to sharing credit and absorbing blame for company results. What he found drives home my point. Fredberg's important conclusions emerged from his study of high-risk, tough-turnaround companies. Here's what he concluded:

> It's no big news that leaders in turnaround situations tend to play a more prominent role in their companies than leaders in business-as-usual scenarios. What's interesting is, in interviews, the CEOs who had led turnarounds took *personal responsibility* when things went wrong and did not hesitate to share the credit with their teams when things went right.
>
> These types of higher-ambition CEOs acknowledge the role they must play as exemplars. They see the willingness to accept personal responsibility—especially

during tough times—as critical to winning the trust of employees and other stakeholders. Leaders, in their view, need the endurance and stamina to lead their organizations through thick and thin. They also need to contain the anxiety of their employees. A leader who spreads the blame, who fails to accept that he or she is ultimately the one in charge, increases the insecurity of their people and lessens the likelihood that they'll take ownership of initiatives.

A leader's individual focus, in other words, is what allows the collective enterprise to flourish . . . the truth . . . seems to be that higher-ambition CEOs assume personal responsibility when things are bad and they give collective credit when things are good. These companies exemplify elements of both strong collective and individual leadership. Both—when used in the right situations—are essential for creating economic as well as social value.[1]

Sharing Credit, Building Partnerships

When working in a partnership with other organizations, credit held onto is credit lost. If sharing the credit for success while willingly assuming the blame for mistakes or failures builds strong teams, the principle is especially true when working across organizational boundaries in partnerships with others. Sharing the credit with a partner organization goes a long way toward forging stronger, more enduring connections that are essential to achieving even more success with additional credits to go around. Effective leaders find ways to place partners in positions of real opportunity for achieving success so that any credit sharing will be authentic and never bogus, manipulative, or inauthentic.

It helps to recognize and to honestly admit that passing along credit even to trusted, essential partners can be challenging. In fact, there are several built-in barriers to successfully sharing credit with partners. Here are a few:

Competition for Funding

Funding the work of your organization can feel overwhelming. If you are the executive leader or the person tasked with raising the capital your team needs to pursue your mission, vying successfully for what appears to be a finite pool of resources can be a daunting task. To be successful in partnerships, you must be willing to take risks in line with your values as a team and an organization. Like the challenge associated with passing the credit along to others, you will face situations surrounding fundraising that will test your character and your courage. Remaining true to your values will eventually pay off, even in a context where funding seems impossible.

Several years ago, at a time when we were a much smaller organization but with aspirations to grow, we received a call from a major bank in the community. The bank had a $500,000 grant to award to a group that worked to develop affordable and permanent supportive housing in our community. My banker friend outlined the conditions of the grant, as well as the bank's intention that the award serve as a catalyst for much-needed housing development in our city. It was exciting just to take his call.

"Larry, where would you invest this fund to achieve the highest impact?" my friend asked me.

We certainly needed the funding.

We were developing housing.

We could make a good case for our receiving the funds.

But our friend at the bank had asked a different question. She wanted to know about highest impact. When we focused on the real issue with honesty, and when we remembered our core values of *stewardship* and *community,* the required, tough answer seemed much easier. We counseled the bank to make an investment in the Corporation for Supportive Housing (CSH) for the good of the larger community and, in this case, for the entire state. Giving credit (literally!) where credit was clearly due cost us in the short run. But it was the right recommendation. And the subsequent success enjoyed by CSH in Texas has been extremely gratifying to watch. I recall this story in an effort to let the pressure off a bit when it comes to competing for funding.

Raising money is one of the hardest jobs in the world. The competition for funds will always be fierce. But by holding on to your predetermined values as the leader of a team, you'll make decisions that display your integrity. Soon word about your team and your organization will spread. Your brand will be served, strengthened, and built.

Over the long haul, funds follow great ideas and trustworthy people. Ironically, the more credit you give away, the more credit you'll receive in return.

In general, we've learned the benefit of celebrating with others in their successes. After all, the point must be the good of the community and success in a worthy mission. Lifting up a so-called competitor will pay off in stronger relationships, shared innovation, and trusted allies who may come to your aid at just the right time further down the line.

Effective, Focused Interface with Media

Reporters almost always operate in urgent space! An essential part of our day-to-day operational strategy insists that we understand the needs and methods of media representatives *before* they show up in our offices, on the phone, with a microphone or behind a camera. Working with media people affords you another opportunity to share the credit for positive results. Directing attention away from yourself and toward your team, your partners, and your funders will always be the path to take whenever you can control the media-shaped environment. The prospect of reporting on some successful venture in the face of a rare challenge draws media quickly. Sharing the credit for breakthroughs at the moment of reporting will serve you and your community well. Just remember: this entire process takes real effort and determined discipline. Simple misunderstandings often occur due to lack of a clearly agreed-upon system and plan for communication.

Often, the reporters you engage won't know enough about your world or the subject at hand, and important details and nuances may be left out of the final report—a special challenge with electronic media. In cases where others need to be credited for good work, talk with team members and partners, both before and after interviews, to make sure they get the credit they deserve. Even after giving reporters all the details and passing along all the credit possible, the final reported product almost always leaves much to be desired. It's just the nature of the business. Preparatory conversations with team members and partners will go a long way to building trust and allowing everyone to assume the best about all partners when the media comes into play.

When reporters come to discuss projects that aren't going so well or raise questions in the community that involve partners or others from our team, we work hard to absorb the negative and deflect any criticism away from our friends. In these cases, executive leadership must be prepared to step up and shoulder whatever negative burden results.

Build a media strategy that majors on full disclosure and open doors for conversation. I seldom turn down a request from the press. It is much better to bring media on than to block them out.

We've found ourselves in the middle of a number of high-profile projects across the years. Giving others credit turns out to be a fun exercise in reality mapping! When we have blown it or when reports haven't come out as we'd like in terms of giving credit to partners, we've been aggressive in explaining to our partners what happened. Overall, we've enjoyed good relations with the press and with partners who've joined us in noteworthy work.

Among the worst mistakes a leader can make is stealing credit from partners and refusing to be open to the press about the success of other organizations. Egocentric leaders go rogue when they grab the credit and run from the interests and questions of the media or, even worse, misrepresent themselves as without peers or partners in any noteworthy project involving many important players.

Failure to Do the Small, Ordinary Things

To maximize the impact of sharing credits, decide now to build strong, authentic working relationships with your team members and your partners. When you share credit, it needs to be real. Nothing fails as miserably as an attempt to share a pseudo credit that's simply not rooted in experience or reality. Make sure you extend wholehearted, authentic credit. In other words, to share credit with a partner, first make sure the partnership is actual.

Ask these questions to gauge the depth and the reality of your partnerships:

- Do you return phone calls to this partner in a timely manner?
- Do you look forward to meetings with this partner?
- Do you take seriously this partner's questions and contributions to the enterprise in question?
- Do you value the work product, the sacrifice, and the commitment of this partner?

- When you share credit with this partner, does it just feel right?

Negative responses to these questions should prompt you to reconsider who your real partners are.

Losing Sight of the Mission and, Thus, Not Planning for Recognition
This sounds ridiculous, but take it from me, it is a genuine concern. Again and again, I need to face the fact that the work I do is not about me. If it ever crosses over that line, I'm off mission. When selfishness rears its small, ugly head, you can be fairly certain that I need to revisit the mission and my understanding and application of my purpose. Mission-focused leaders share credit freely. Properly understood and pursued, our mission drives, shapes, forms, and defines the work of the organization. It is from that basis that the distribution of credit becomes a natural part of the culture of any organization. When I'm excited about our mission, rather than my own reputation or status, I find sharing credit a completely natural, enjoyable endeavor.

For example, if my mission relates to eliminating the food deserts that stretch across Dallas County, I will be drawn to others who share this objective. When a team member or a community partner effectively drives a process for success in completing this mission, I will find it easy and necessary to extend credit and cheer on my partners in this mission. On the other hand, if I work in this field but have a different mission, especially a self-serving mission rather than the mission I claim, chances are I'm not going to be very concerned about giving others credit for their work.

Forget recognition.
Pursue your mission.
Celebrate others.

Your Turn

1. Consider a time when you freely extended credit to a member of your team. How did it feel? How did the recipient of your praise react? What motivated you to share the credit?
2. Consider a time when you shared the credit with a partner outside your organization. How did it feel? How did your partner react? Did sharing credit result in anything you could report?
3. Now, think of a time when someone gave you credit for work well done or for special effort. How did it make you feel? How did it affect your performance going forward?
4. What do leaders need to learn about sharing credit? Explain.
5. On a scale of 1 to 10, with 10 being most clear, how clear are you on your organization's mission? What do you need to do with this evaluation?
6. As a team, how freely do you and your teammates share credit with one another? With partners? Why?
7. Do you work in a culture of credit sharing? Explain. How could you do better at this?

NOTE

[1] Tobias Fredberg, "Why Good Leaders Pass the Credit and Take the Blame," *Harvard Business Review*, October 6, 2011, https://hbr.org/2011/10/why-good -leaders-pass-the-cred.

CHAPTER SIX

PATIENT WITH PEOPLE; IMPATIENT WITH PROBLEMS

Patience among leaders builds effective teams.

Patience in the face of obstacles, setbacks, and disappointments often results in amazing breakthroughs. Patience involves endurance against seemingly long odds—odds that can appear to be growing longer the further you go into a project, a challenge, or a problem without evidence of success. Patience calls up perseverance, steadfastness in mission. Patience provides strength and courage to the extent that the patient leader or team member never seriously or for very long considers the notion of quitting or giving up.

At the same time, patience often means forgiveness—forgiving team members, partners, and investors. What good comes from patience—when confronted with obstacles—that doesn't translate to understanding and forbearance when others fail or let us down?

Patience serves as the glue that holds teams, projects, and organizations together whenever leaders take seriously the other principles discussed in this book. Anyone fortunate enough to watch patient leaders and team members at work almost always walks away with feelings of inspiration, respect, and admiration. Self-awareness and clarity about your own weaknesses help in the process of extending patience to others.

A "Killer" Project

Tough projects call for truckloads of patience.

Without a doubt, the toughest project I've ever worked through resulted in the development of the Cottages at Hickory Crossing in Dallas. Without going into all the difficult, gory details, let me point out the patience-trying, major elements of the challenging effort. In 2009, we pulled together a group of collaborative partners, including a strong, local foundation; the county's criminal justice system; our housing development division; the premier mental health provider in the county; professors at the medical school who signed on to measure our outcomes; the City of Dallas; a local nonprofit architectural firm; an outside consulting company; and CitySquare.

The foundation provided a generous, "first in" matching grant. The remaining partners helped raise the funds needed to plan, design, site, build, and operate a new neighborhood consisting of fifty small homes built for fifty of the homeless people who cost the most for Dallas County. We calculated that each of the fifty residents who would occupy the housing cost the county well over $40,000 annually while remaining homeless on our streets and under our bridges. Once housed in the new development and surrounded by high-touch, concierge services and high-quality mental health care, each resident's costs were well below $15,000 annually. The homes provided 400 square feet of living space that included a living room, bedroom, kitchen, dining area, and full bathroom, as well as a sizable front porch that opened to five or six other front porches.

Great project, right? Absolutely. But with interesting qualifiers!

Every aspect of the joint effort soon turned complicated, tiring, and extremely complex. The design process tested the partnership. The architects loved the project and its innovative style. Some partners wondered if it was too complicated, but the group patiently held on. A now-humorous detail involves the fact that the project won a prestigious American Institute of Architects award for the best "unbuilt" project of the year. We've had lots of laughs over that one! There were moments when I felt the award may have frozen us in time as we worked through turning the plan from unbuilt to completed.

Funding presented additional problems and challenges. Before we could start, the funding had to be secured, and it took us about five years to line up what we needed. Metrocare saved us by holding a large note on a necessary loan that we secured early on in the project. Purchasing the land had its moments. Impatience with our developer waxed and waned, as the leaders determined to hang tough for a project the city needed so badly.

On more than one occasion, I descended on the jobsite with fire in my eyes, projecting anything but a patient presence. One of my visits turned so negative that some feared the general contractor would leave the jobsite. Clearly, the project demonstrated my own fierce impatience. Why is it that self-understanding arrives in waves after incidents of failure or poor performance?

The project reached a breaking point in 2013–2014 when most partners grew extremely weary of the process and its various complicating factors. Maybe this was just too hard. At that crucial juncture, a couple of partners asked the larger group to stand down for a bit and allow them to make one last push at assembling the capital necessary to complete the project. The other partners eagerly agreed. After several months and lots of focused work, with some-old fashioned luck or divine intervention thrown in for good measure, the funds arrived and the project moved toward the finish line.

Big win, right? Not exactly!

A series of real problems confronted us. Not only did 2015 turn out to be the wettest year in the history of Texas, we faced delays, construction material problems, general contractor deficiencies, labor shortages, challenges constructing the cool but difficult-to-assemble buildings, polite but real internal conflict among the partners, as well as finding the potential tenants and making sure they cued up in a timely fashion for moving in when the building phase of the project wrapped up.

We finally managed to complete the construction. We moved in all fifty of the residents into their new homes in January 2017. The project took a lot to complete. The main ingredient for success in the end, every day and at every turn: old-fashioned patience.

Exercising patience takes good care of people, especially partners and teammates. Defaulting to patience in trying situations, while not always easy, automatic, or popular, results in deepened connections and resilient partnerships. Patience, when embraced as an internal discipline, allows for negotiation, calming crisis, and movement forward, even in the toughest of times or circumstances. Resorting to patience builds community. Patient responses prompt the emergence of stories that, if allowed room for growth, shape culture and assign deeper meaning to important efforts. When you feel the need to calm down and wait on behalf of another person, you find yourself in the deep spaces provided by the presence of patience.

Leading from the Middle

There is no accounting for the number of times people asked us, "When will the cottages open?" To say the least, that question grew extremely tiresome. But the question was legitimate in view of the varied interests of our partners, investors, and residents—wonderful people who badly needed housing options and good solutions. I began to regard that question as an opportunity for growth in patience, endurance, and blameless regard for others, even those who created many of the delays. I've learned that being patient often places a leader in the lonely middle ground between honest critics (usually a step removed from the issue at hand) and the source that fuels their impatience. The patient leader will learn to spend her time brokering progress between and among conflicting interests and perspectives. Working in this middle ground is not easy. On the one hand, the leader supports the concerns of the critics to the person, organization, or people whose actions create stressful circumstances. On the other, an effective leader interprets the disappointments and the forces beyond anyone's control that create counterproductive impatience. This is the hard, demanding work of conflict management that every leader must embrace. If we failed in any fundamental way as we worked through this difficult project, it was in not communicating more with everyone involved. Included among the many important lessons learned was the necessity of developing a communications strategy before any project begins. Such a plan deserves a place in the concept development stage!

In fact, though, fretting, acting rudely, and focusing frustration and impatience on others usually gets us nowhere.

Patience in tough situations sharpens focus. Patience protects your greatest, most essential catalytic asset: your people and your brand reputation. Patience enhances your brand in a community as an organization or leader who gets things done, even difficult things. Patience is a prerequisite for progress. Being patient with people generally pays big social and relational dividends. And, for the record, The Cottages have earned encouraging recognition.[1]

The Place for Impatience

While being impatient with others ought to be avoided, being impatient with problems, deficiencies, circumstances, policies, and conditions will often be required. In fact, experiencing and expressing impatience with problems is an essential mark of transformative leaders and organizations. Nothing justifies patience with

generational poverty
homelessness
inaccessibility to living wage work
injustice in social and political systems and in relationships
institutionalized systems that produce inequity
hunger
chronic disease
substandard educational opportunities
segregation
public leaders who don't lead justly
neighborhood gatekeepers who block progress
racism
spousal abuse
exploitation
opportunity gaps
child abuse
discrimination
people and systems that engage in, promote, and sustain
    such social maladies

Mission awareness and commitment to a big cause, involving high stakes for others, force you to be impatient with hurtful problems and pressing issues. At times, what appears to be impatience with people is actually a "line in the sand" moment where decisive, bold, courageous action is required. Dr. Martin Luther King Jr. exhibited love for everyone, even his enemies, in some of the most trying of circumstances. He taught us much about the creation of the "beloved community." King could be patient with people, even his fiercest critics and opponents.

At the same time, King mounted a compelling campaign against racism, discrimination, and the crippling injustice that crushed the poor of his generation. He always loved people, but he moved with unforgiving impatience against the problems of his day. King's "Letter from Birmingham Jail" contains one of his most influential exhibitions of clear, justifiable impatience with the state of affairs for African Americans in the United States. Sadly, too often we get it backward. We remain patient with the causes and effects of injustice, while withholding patience from the people around us who are doing their best every day while living in our racist system. At the end of his life, King joined arms with striking sanitation workers in Memphis, Tennessee, to express his unflinching impatience toward a failed system in need of reform and radical renewal, rather than the oppressive business-as-usual approach that he could not tolerate.

Building a strong organization grounded in a commitment both to justice and friendship can get complicated. Often, the high-wire balancing act stretches between the two values. Friendship calls us to refine our skills in ways that encourage growth in patience. Justice prompts us to stand up strongly and with urgency for fairness and systemic equity. To be very practical (and honest), funding usually follows friendship and good ideas, both of which encourage patience and deepening understanding among part-ners. But concerns for equity and justice have a way of coming up and factoring into timing decisions and the uncompromised practice of fundamental organizational values. Working along this challenging continuum calls for both unwavering patience in practice and unmixed courage in decision-making.

Your Turn

1. How do you know when it is time to be impatient? Can you list four to five signals that tell you it's time for impatience?
2. Consider a time when you expressed your impatience with a member of your team. How did it feel? How did the person with whom you were impatient react? Why were you impa-tient? Could you have done better as a leader in this situation? How?
3. Consider a time when you became impatient with a partner outside your organization. How did it feel? How did your partner react? Did you honestly discuss your impatience and its cause?
4. Now, think of a time when someone became impatient with you. How did it make you feel? How did it affect your perfor-mance going forward?
5. What do leaders need to learn about impatience? Explain your opinions.
6. As a team, how freely do you and your teammates confess your impatience with one another? With partners? How can you improve?
7. Do you and your organization work in a culture of impa-tience? When justified; when not? Explain.

8. When was the last time you impatiently challenged a real, human-crushing reality? How do you justify your impatience? How was your impatience expressed?
9. How is your mission related to what makes you feel impatient? Explain.
10. What have you discovered in your life and work that needs to be challenged with "holy impatience"?

NOTE

[1] John Cary, *Design for Good: A New Era of Architecture for Everyone* (Washington, DC: Island Press, 2017), 104-12.

CHAPTER SEVEN

EXPECT RESULTS

It's not enough to try hard. Something must change because of your effort.

Organizations that resist measurement should be questioned.

For the last several years, CitySquare has used a software product with a useful "dashboard" format for reporting outcomes. It documents how each of our various efforts do indeed result in beneficial outcomes for our neighbors so that we can communicate these reports clearly to our program leaders, donors, and contracting agencies.

Report cards matter. Organizations that resist measurement and evaluation don't deserve support or endorsement. Funders expect results, and they should because our neighbors deserve results, real results that change lives in ways that matter.

Outputs versus Outcomes

At the same time, it is important to recognize the difference in our units of measurement. Program outputs aren't the same as outcomes. The distinction is extremely important. Outputs tend to measure the elements of effort, the activities of people. Outcomes measure substantive change, real-life results—hopefully the results of outputs being applied to the problems at hand. A neighborhood food pantry could be expected to report pounds of food distributed to those in need. That is reporting on outputs. And it is an important measure. But to measure the impact of the food distributed, you must focus on outcomes. Outcome reporting measures the human benefit and life change in areas such as documented nutritional improvements, increased household wealth or income, and enhanced health and well-being. And all must be measured against reasonable standards that indicate success and progress.

If you ever wonder about the difference between outputs and outcome, ask this question: Of the various initiatives that I'm concerned about measuring in terms of the impact of my work, which ones are harder to report on? Chances are the more difficult something is to report, the more important it turns out to be for your work and the more in line it is with outcomes rather than far simpler outputs or units of service.

Outcome reporting is not easy, simple, or automatic. Typically, outcome reports end up focusing on smaller sets of the population you serve. For example, in a workforce training program, you may report that in the first quarter of the year, you enrolled and trained one hundred students in an orientation to construction trades course. That is an output report. But if you've devised a way to capture initial employment success for seventy-three of these one hundred graduates, you are now reporting a useful outcome. If you are able to go further by tracking students over their first year following your training program and can report that sixty-one of the original one hundred secured and held employment for a year, that's even better. If you can monetize the real worth of the jobs maintained for a year to the student's real income and to any local, state, or federal taxing system, you're moving further in the direction of reporting genuine impact.

Or take permanent housing for formerly homeless people. Building or funding housing units for the extremely poor results in a large capital investment by donors, funders, and organizations. In this case, the number of housing units provided and the "per door cost" would be an important output to report. Even more powerful would be to compare the costs associated with being homeless to the costs associated with having a place to call home. Study after study reveals that a significant savings in public and private funds occurs after people move off the streets and into permanent homes. The outcome in cost reduction alone is startling. Drilling down even deeper into health outcomes, criminal justice system avoidance, and overall well-being, the results astonish us.

Almost by definition, delivering evidence-based programming to attack poverty will raise tough questions related to scale. The work being done to train and retrain a twenty-first-century workforce is demanding and hard work. Results relate directly to funding, program capacity, numbers of programs, available venues, and teacher proficiency. Often, the reporting from these labor intensive and expensive efforts will surprise donors or funders who may not be well informed as to the challenges of the work performed. Such a reality makes gathering outcome data even more important. Collected outcomes, if used properly, serve as tools for the education of funders and potential partners. Once informed and educated, funders and collaborators can begin to respond in more reasonable and helpful ways to address the challenges we face.

We've learned to use a "dashboard" approach to regularly report our data. We also use stories that exemplify not only our best work, but our typical work. Combining dashboard data by area with the stories that arise from our work seems to be an effective way to tell the CitySquare story. In thank-you letters to generous donors, we often print photos with brief stories of the neighbors who visit our various locations. The combination of gratitude, overall feedback on our efforts, and a typical story works well in the important work of keeping us all together.

As noted already, outcome reporting presents real challenges. Such reporting takes time. It is tedious by its very nature. Legitimate outcome reporting costs. Dealing with data isn't always fun. If you can find ways to humanize and personalize the process, your efforts will be more successful and significant. And developing a culture that expects outcome reporting as standard operating procedure will pay off big time for the neighbors you engage and the funders on whom you count. To become proficient at the skill and process of measuring results in hard, real-world terms, effort will be required. Fortunately, lots of helpful training is available to leaders and teams. Much useful material can be found online. Organizations, even start-ups, can benefit greatly by giving due attention to the matter of measuring impact and success.[1]

Friendship

How do we measure the impact of friendship on what we accomplish? Many data purists would regard the question as largely irrelevant. However, we've found friendship to be an integral part of our entire community development strategy. Friendship falls into the category of "soft outcomes." But we've found that without a positive personal relationship with our neighbors, the outcomes we seek elude us. Of course, friendship, mutual respect, confidence in a coach, joy in the process of progress, and many other human connections defy measurement. Friendship as an essential asset may be hard to adequately define or place in a logic model, but you know it when you watch it developing and transforming people. One of the reasons we insist on improving our ability to measure and report real changes is the fact that we're dealing with friends, whether teacher or student. The power of friendship is so crucial, so essential to us, that we include it as part of our mission at CitySquare.

Friendship drives us toward better, improved program performance. The people who visit our food center are our friends and customers. They matter deeply in all that we do. Because of our friendship, we look at numbers differently. Every number reports on a friend or a group of our friends. So numbers matter to us, and we pay attention to them.

Quality of life matters. We pay attention to these concerns because of the people involved—people who are precious to us. The men and women who live in the housing we provide and manage report astounding results in terms of housing retention, income improvement, and overall well-being and stability. While it is true that we have great professionals who work with us in our housing efforts, equally important is the culture of friendship that is just a part of what we like to call "the CitySquare Way." Deep relationships cause us to pay careful attention to the data. Change for the better and progress along a disciplined pathway matter to us. We celebrate with our friends when the numbers reflect this progress. We become concerned and reconsider our efforts if the numbers move in the opposite direction.

Inherent in every process, program, procedure, and activity is room for improvement and advancement for everyone involved. This value commitment should be multidimensional, as well as simultaneous. For example, a neighbor's need for the services of our food program may signal her need for training that leads to a better job that pays a living wage. But the food center team must also continually be considering the challenges associated with their work. While directing a single mother to better income, the food team must also pursue the daily mission of finding ways to have more impact with food. We can do food better, as well as all our other community offerings.

Friendship teaches us that our results shouldn't be defined by the expectations of the "helping class," but by consumer expectations that remain grounded in respect and genuine partnership. Friendship continually motivates us to measure outcomes and impact. That's the case because so much is at stake for our friends and our community.

But friendship matters far more than most of us typically realize. In fact, a growing body of research argues that a major cause that drives people to addictive behaviors is the absence of meaningful relationships. In short, people living without the benefit of a genuine community of real friends battle addictions. Drug addiction follows loneliness and isolation. The chemical realities of addictive behavior do not explain the process leading up to and out of drug, alcohol, and sexual addictions. Johann Hari reported on amazing findings of research into the causes behind addiction in his groundbreaking book *Chasing the Scream: The First and Last Days of the War on Drugs*:

> Human beings have a deep need to bond and form connections. It's how we get our satisfaction. If we can't connect with each other, we will connect with anything we can find—the whirr of a roulette wheel or the prick of a syringe. He says we should stop talking about "addiction" altogether, and instead call it "bonding." A heroin addict has bonded with heroin because she couldn't bond as fully with anything else. So the opposite of addiction is not sobriety. It is human connection.[2]

Years ago at CitySquare, as noted already, we placed "friendship" in our mission statement: "CitySquare fights the causes and effects of poverty through direct service, advocacy, and friendship." We did that because we recognized and witnessed the power of human connection, friendship, and community in our work. What applies to our team certainly applies equally to our neighbors, the customers who show up every day to engage and with whom we work directly. The spirit of our organization permeates our growing community.

In the end, our "secret sauce" is simple friendship.

Your Turn

1. Consider for a moment an organization that's important to you. Do you know if this group measures and evaluates its impact and/or success? If so, how do you know, and what are the results?
2. How important is measuring and evaluating performance to you? Why? "We measure what matters." Do you agree with this statement? Why or why not?
3. How motivated would you be if you were asked to direct your funding to the expense of measuring outcomes in the organizations you support? Explain.
4. How do you feel about friendship and its importance in community development? Explain.

NOTES

[1] The Compassion Capital Fund, U.S. Department of Health and Human Services, *Strengthening Nonprofits: A Capacity Builder's Resource Library,* http://strengtheningnonprofits.org/resources/Guidebooks/MeasuringOutcomes.pdf.

[2] Johann Hari, "The Likely Cause of Addiction Has Been Discovered, and It Is Not What You Think," *Huffington Post,* January 20, 2015, http://www.huffingtonpost.com/johann-hari/the-real-cause-of-addicti_b_6506936.html.

CHAPTER EIGHT

INTERPRET PEOPLE— LISTEN

Theological education prepares students in the exegesis of biblical texts. To ascertain the meaning of an ancient passage, students commit themselves to studying original languages, the social contexts of the authors, the historical surroundings, and contemporary events relating to matters from the mundane to the esoteric. The broad sweep and the deep reach of understanding necessary to interpret the documents of one of the major historic religions of the world provides parallel principles for understanding or, better, interpreting people.

Complex social and community problems call for dedicated leaders and team members who possess great integrity, resourcefulness, and ingenuity. To be effective as community builders, we must learn the valuable skills necessary to understand others, to interpret the lives they present, along with their actions, attitudes, traditions, experiences, history, and values. The leader who learns the fine art of "people exegesis" will find new ability to affect meaningful changes that allow diverse groups of people to achieve more with this intimate knowledge of others than could be attained without it.

What I have in view here relates to work done in defining and analyzing the relatively new field of understanding of social intelligence. In this regard, Robert Greene is probably correct when he observes, "Your work is the single greatest means at your disposal for expressing your social intelligence."[1]

But here I want to focus on just one essential trait or skill absolutely essential for leaders who understand the benefit of "interpreting" or understanding their teams.

One Essential Skill for Interpreting People

Are you ready?

Here it is: listen closely.

You got it?

Let me repeat it: listen closely.

That's right. To understand others, you must make a serious commitment to listening, and listening carefully. In every encounter, resist the ever-present temptation to rush into your agenda. We've all been there, talking to a person who won't listen because he's too busy formulating a reply. We all can recall how that feels, can't we?

Take the time to reconstruct the personal life context of your teammates and others whom you seek to influence and bring along on your mission. Learning as much as possible about their development, experience, and history will be essential in forming relationships that deliver transformation all around. Nothing communicates respect for another person like genuine interest in their story.

Recognize that few experiences encourage others quite as much as when a leader or a colleague inquires about the life dynamics and experiences that make a person who he is today. If I sense that you care about my story and about what my life means in my view, I will quickly consider you a friend and an ally. In genuine listening, leaders will discover amazing power among those they seek to lead and direct. The experience of being listened to is so unique that when discovered, a person tends to lock in on the one who provides the wonderful gift of an attentive ear. In fact, we've all had the experience of hearing others report on the good listeners in the group, the organization, the family, or the circle of common interest.

Listening Can Be Directed with Purpose

To get to know others at a depth below the surface, we will need to learn how to ask "value-based" questions—questions that open up the intimate world of the person I need to understand and interpret if I am to be an effective leader with authentic concern for my team. Such questions may relate to faith, politics, devotion, commitments, personal passions, group involvement, family, upbringing, education, loss, achievement, disappointments, encouragements, setbacks, life geography, and countless other dimensions in the personal life of the person I seek, above all, to understand.

Listen as an Organizer and Play-Caller

If I interpret those around me correctly, I gain understanding about how to order my team. Knowing the things that matter most to team members allows me to place people where they will have the best chance to be successful and productive. If I know what experiences have shaped the person I seek to understand, and why and how these formative life experiences matter so much, I have a real possibility to engage the other person productively for his sake, the team's sake, as well as my sake as a leader who will be held accountable.

Listening and Understanding Others Deeply

Be a leader who regards listening as an essential tool for understanding others deeply. All sorts of professional tools exist for identifying personality types. Similar instruments are available for determining various professional and personal aptitudes. Other programs gauge temperament, relational styles, diverse leadership assessment, and even spiritual orientations. Undoubtedly, these tools prove useful in better understanding yourself and your team.

Clear Benefits of "Deep and Careful Listening"

Don't forget, however, that one of the most effective tools of all, available to you in virtually every situation in which you find yourself, is simply to listen. On a daily basis, you can place yourself at the disposal of other people and receive the messages they value in a way that allows you to interpret them for their own sakes and for the benefit of your team.

- Deep and careful listening focuses attention and opens up the leader's eyes and mind to receive nonverbal messages or body language.
- Deep and careful listening helps identify the various nuances contained in another person's words.
- Deep and careful listening enables leaders to connect the dots in another person's life, and almost always leads to clarifying questions.
- Deep and careful listening promotes true understanding and leads the way to necessary compromise.

- Deep and careful listening opens up opportunities and options for improvement and even advancement on the team—both for the leader and the led.
- Deep and careful listening helps leaders make strategic changes, as leaders from the front lines feel free to speak freely, knowing their words won't be wasted or unheeded.
- Deep and careful listening communicates your respect for the person talking. Respect builds successful, confident, productive teams.

Your Turn

1. Do you consider yourself to be a good listener? Why or why not?
2. Have you personally observed the impact listening or being heard has on others? Give an example.
3. How important to a team's culture is a leader who genuinely listens? Explain.
4. How do you feel when you know another person is not listening to you? What does not being heard communicate to you?
5. How do you feel about friendship and its importance in community development? Explain.

NOTE

[1]Robert Greene, *Mastery* (London: Penguin, 2012), 152.

CHAPTER NINE

SEE THE TREASURE

No matter where a leader finds herself, if she is attuned to reality and even the least bit astute, she will soon discover that treasure surrounds her—human treasure.

Often, talented people find themselves misplaced in an organization. Or community folks find themselves sequestered in a stereotypical role that prevents them from rising to exert and exercise their real wealth. How many administrative assistants or line staff members on your own team feel the freedom to engage and act through the talent they know that they possess? Too often, real talent gets tucked away in places where no one can take proper notice. To see and seize upon the wealth of all the people we encounter, lead, hire, and place, a determined cultural shift must take place. And the new culture must at least be welcomed by those who lead. No lesson has been so clearly impressed upon my life as the truth that all people, all team members, and all customers with whom you work have treasure to spend in the enterprise of your organization, church, business, nonprofit, or classroom.[1]

Years ago, while working in the food pantry at CitySquare, I met a neighbor, Willie Jackson, who taught me the important lessons I needed to learn about valuing the contributions the very poor could make to our growing organization. Willie needed a home. He came to us from the streets in a fairly desperate situation. I first met him when he slept behind our building. As we got acquainted, I learned that he had a problem with cocaine. He didn't try to hide his struggle from me. At the same time, I learned that he was an accomplished carpenter. The more we talked and the more he volunteered in our food distribution center, the more we came to trust and rely upon each other. Willie needed a place to stay. I needed someone to build a group of small conference rooms in our interview facility. We also needed painting, upkeep, and additional modifications to our building. So, Willie and I struck up a deal. I hired him to do the work, paid him a fair wage, and allowed him to live in our center until the work was completed. The entire arrangement worked out well. He performed the needed work. We provided him a bridge out of homelessness and addiction. The partnership worked. Willie proved himself as an invaluable treasure to our organization.

To find human capital, one must first believe that it exists. If you enter your day not expecting to run into treasure in human form, chances are you won't discover it. But, if you're willing to shift paradigms to recognize different ways of operating, you will stand a much better chance of finding exactly what you need, and at the same time, you'll open a door for another person to use, to invest his real value in your enterprise in such a way that everyone benefits.

Sometimes people stubbornly bring their capital to a community and invest it there without being invited. My friend Pat lives in a shelter in South Dallas. She works every day, but no one pays her. You'll see her out on the streets of her community with her broom, her large dustpan, and her trash can on wheels. She sweeps the sidewalks, driveways, and gutters. She picks up the trash and cans. She wears overalls and a bright orange and yellow safety vest. She works extremely hard. I don't know everything about Pat, but I do know she's had a hard life involving lots of abuse, the kind that saps your soul of optimism and hope. But the specifics of her undeclared struggles don't deter her from productive work for the benefit of all who live and work in the community. Everyone knows Pat. Everyone calls out to her as they pass by on foot, on the bus, or in cars. A few observations remain constant about Pat. She always smiles. She stays at the work that is hers and hers alone. She remains content and purposeful. The value of her work in the community from a public health and safety perspective is undeniable. Pat is a pure treasure. Her spirit reflects the reality that everyone has so much to offer. Pat has found her way to invest her treasure. We have a real opportunity to mobilize countless other people like Pat with real treasure to offer up for the betterment and healing of our neighborhoods.

Most of us with money to invest look for clear returns on our investments. We limit ourselves by relying on only investments involving paper transactions. Money is only one form of wealth. We discover treasure when we trust enough to invest in people.

Years ago, a family who regularly volunteered for us went on to become vital members of our community. The father in the family worked hard, though he lacked the documents he needed to secure "legal" employment. As a result, his wages remained low and represented only a fraction of the value of his efforts to his employer. The family included three children when we first met. We became well-acquainted over time. Late one Friday afternoon, the father knocked at my office door. I greeted this man and his young son who had come along to translate our conversation. He asked if we could visit. I told him that we could. What followed was a long explanation of the fact that his oldest son remained in Mexico, but the family was prepared to welcome him to their home so that the family could be reunited after several years of difficult separation. As we spoke, I wondered what sort of pain and discouragement must have been endured by everyone in the family for such a long time.

When we got to the bottom line, the father asked me for $900 to make the trip to Mexico and back, including expense money to get back into the United States once he connected with his son. I remember thinking to myself as I made the necessary arrangements to deliver the cash he requested, *would I be any different if I was in his position, separated from one of my children?* Of course, I knew that I would be exactly like my friend. About six weeks later, I heard another knocking on my door. When I opened the door, there was the father with his oldest son, who had arrived from Mexico. The man paid us back over time, in volunteer hours and in cash. Reflecting on the entire situation, I'm sure I've never made a better investment.

In fact, the story doesn't end there. Our investment tapped into the treasure trove of this family's wealth. As the reunited son grew, he joined our summer youth staff, working in a real job that paid real wages. He studied with our staff and became proficient in computer hardware and software. He became a real leader in his community and his church. Eventually, he joined our staff at CitySquare. He married and today is the proud father of three young sons. No, I'm certain I've never made a better investment paid back several times over in the treasure that is this family. A huge part of the dividend on the investment included the treasure of community knowledge, social capital, and leadership freely offered up by this wonderful family to all members of our community.

At times, the treasure you should be looking to discover will involve vital community research and understanding. Once your team members realize that you as the leader remain constantly on the lookout for talent, knowledge, and the treasure of new, innovative, relevant ideas, you'll be surprised at what you discover right under your nose.

Over twenty years ago, after we started seriously listening to our customers, they informed us of the community's need for legal representation in civil law courts. We took the knowledge shared by our friends, and we treated it like treasure. The result of this feedback: the founding of a public interest law firm. Had we not been on the lookout for the valuable understanding provided by the community of our customers, the law firm would not exist today, leaving thousands of people unrepresented at the bar of justice in our community.

Joe Wesson was a friend of mine for about five years before he passed away following a hard struggle with cancer. Joe knew tough times. He lived on the streets of South Dallas for over a decade. I'm not sure that I've ever known a tougher guy than Joe. Joe was a fighter. I first met him on the corner of Malcolm X Boulevard and Louise Street. He chided me in the early days of our friendship because for the life of me, I couldn't remember his name. Finally, I mastered that. Joe became the unofficial outside eyes/night watchman over one of our major construction projects. He reported whenever anyone visited our building site after hours. He even witnessed the theft of a large air compressor and trailer, a crime he reported in amazing detail. Joe kept us posted on everything happening in the community. He finally secured permanent housing, but then faced the diagnosis of brain cancer. Joe passed away in a hospice center following his last surgery. Joe could be downright ornery and, at times, alarmingly pugnacious, but he played an unusual but essential role in our community, an example of a person who contributed the treasure of his keen eyes and his overall savvy about our community.

How to Win the Treasure Hunt

Again, to find valuable human assets, you must be on the lookout as a natural part of your plan for leading your organization or community. Not only do your eyes need to be open to everything, the same must be said for your mind and your evaluation process. Here are a few things I've discovered in playing the human capital treasure hunt:

- *Anticipate people of value.* Expect to find real, often tangible value in people, especially in the members of your team and the community where you work. Set a cultural expectation that values all the people with whom you work, serve, and encounter. Train your managers in the fine art of observing breakthrough ideas or suggestions and "Aha!" moments.

- *Measure the value of the treasure you discover.* Assign measureable worth to the people you mobilize for the good of your mission. If they are volunteers, use recognized standards for per hour value for these essential team members. Find ways to document and to recognize what your measures prove.

- *Tell the story that your data illustrates.* Make it an ironclad policy to document what you discover as you mine your community's assets. Record hours served. Calculate the number of people engaged by your teams. Assess how many people with whom you connect might become valued members of your professional staff. As you develop the discipline to measure the quality and depth of your community talent, you will be pleasantly surprised with the numbers and the results of the work performed by valuable community teammates.

- *Employ community members whenever and wherever you can.* Given what you know about the treasure community people bring to a task and to challenges, plan to employ them as much as possible.
- *Shake folks up periodically.* Have team games that include job switches and team work shuffles that are designed to cross-train your employees. Build "innovation conversations" that embed cross-functional endeavors into your culture and strategic planning. In the process, you will allow team members to understand at a deeper level the various aspects of the work you accomplish together. Do all of this with a keen eye to the new ideas you can bank in your ever-expanding treasure chest.
- *Trust in the newly discovered treasure of your team.* Spend the sustained wealth as your community of thinking innovators decide. As you discover the heretofore hidden treasure, celebrate the wealth.

Your Turn

1. How good are you at discovering treasure in others with whom you work, lead, and follow? Why do you say that?
2. Have you discovered real treasure in the life of another person with whom you worked? What happened?
3. What questions do you have about mining treasure from community people who appear to possess anything but treasure? How do our limited definitions of treasure/wealth curtail us in finding treasure buried in the lives and talents of others?

4. What happens in an organization that expects to find treasure in everyone?
5. When have your treasure hunts failed? Tell a story about this.

NOTE

[1]See my previous book, *The Wealth of the Poor: How Valuing Every Neighbor Restores Hope in Our Cities* (Abilene, TX: Abilene Christian University Press, 2013).

CHAPTER TEN

FIND JOY

What does joy have to do with work?

I mean, doesn't the Bible say that work is a curse imposed on us for our fundamental failure to pursue selfless truth and trust in our creator (or something like that)? For sure, work can become a real curse, the ultimate bummer! Yet, I've found that when a person or a group aligns life and values around a worthwhile— even noble—mission, joy results. If the mission is right and if the right people pursue that purpose with "all in," reckless, sacrificial abandon, joy will not be hard to find, nurture, and thoroughly experience! Like the Wisdom Writer shares, "When justice is done, it brings joy to the righteous but terror to evildoers" (Prov. 21:15).

I've witnessed this phenomenon across many sectors of the world of work. You name the field, almost every endeavor holds out the possibility of an important return of motivating joy in work accomplished.

How do we find joy as we battle injustice, poverty, and the darkness of the attendant realities we face every day? At times, finding joy can be a tough assignment. Over the years, I have realized that my determined search for motivation to continue the work I do must be grounded in the special delight of joy. Joy, at least as I understand it, acts like a steroid injection relieving pain in calcified joints, tried and tired by the fight of our work. When recognized, an experience of joy rushes relief to weary people in need of respite and hope.

Hope and joy seem to be siblings. Just when I feel the most hopeless, an experience of joy revives my heart and my strength. I've learned that opportunities for experiencing joy are planted all around and throughout my community. For me, the challenge with joy is all about attentiveness to it and its many surprises.

People are almost always the delivery service employed by joy. And joy usually comes wrapped in deep appreciation and love. When I love my community and all its people, joy shows up for me.

When I feel joy sliding by me, I've learned to stop and take stock of the fundamental motivation behind the work I attempt. Duty and a sense of obligation carry me only so far. Love must become for us the wellspring of inspiring joy. I'm moved by the experience of Albert Einstein:

> From the age of six to fourteen I took violin lessons but had no luck with my teachers, for whom music did not transcend mechanical practicing. I really began to learn only after I had fallen in love with Mozart's sonatas. The attempt to reproduce their singular grace compelled me to improve my technique. I believe, on the whole, that love is a better teacher than sense of duty.[1]

Where Do I Find Joy?

So where do I find joy for the work I do? Where should I set up camp for experiencing the refreshment of joy? Consider these tips.

Stay Close to People Who Successfully Bring Their Faith against Oppression

Somewhere in their motivation to work and stay at their work for the sake of equity and justice, you'll find plenty of opportunity for joyous living. The entire enterprise of seeking justice involves working closely with people and getting to know them, their struggles, their deepest feelings, and, at times, their most intimate secrets and fears. Organizing communities in working for a more just society creates the bonds of human connection that periodically erupt into all-out, pure joy! Whenever we work for justice, sooner or later a party will break out. Working for justice, for fairness, for equal opportunity and uniform options, means that my closest friends will be with me in the struggle, no matter its cost, form, or outcome.

Over the years, I've worked with a number of groups devoted to the realization of social justice. Battling usury in our efforts to regulate payday lending in Texas or working to eliminate hunger via the Texas Hunger Initiative or pressing for health-care reform or advocating for full funding for our public schools, in every case I've witnessed expressions of deep joy in the lives of almost everyone involved.

Realize That Joy Is Not the Product of Material Wealth or the Accumulation of Things

Joy proceeds from a deep place in the human soul, a place satisfied only by movement toward the realization of peace, harmony, and human connection. Increasing my net worth will not bring me joy. Deepening my connection to people delivers joy. Working for the overall benefit of my community sets up opportunity after opportunity for the experience of joy. Sooner or later, joy always follows authentic human connection.

Terry, one of my friends who battles extreme poverty, earns his living by doing card tricks on the downtown sidewalks of Dallas. He is a master magician when manipulating a deck of playing cards. I first met him as I walked down a Deep Ellum street with friends. He asked me if I would like to see one of his tricks. I answered that I would. From that point, Terry and I developed our friendship. His life story fascinates me as he unwinds detail after detail in our continuing conversation as friends. We've enjoyed lots of laughter, story after story of our experiences, and just the good stuff of being friends. Terry turns out to be a political junky and one of the most well-informed people I've ever met, reading the newspaper from front to back on a daily basis, whenever he can afford to purchase a copy.

Terry brings me joy.

He came by my office not long ago to ask a favor. Terry doesn't panhandle or beg, so a request from him was unusual. He insists on working for his living using his cards. His request was not for money, but for assistance in obtaining a copy of his birth certificate—a process I find much more onerous than is necessary. In the ordeal of working to get the document he needed, I learned even more about him. Born in Greenville, Texas, a son in a tight and successful family, Terry bottomed out for a good while after the death of his mother. Lost in his grief, he came to Dallas and hit the tough streets. He continues to tell me that we need to document his life story and make a movie. From what I'm learning, he's likely right about that.

Once, he offered a great compliment that brought me real joy.

"Larry, you see, man, I trust you. You're my friend, so I figure I can tell you my story, and you'll take care of it."

For sure, I've found great joy in this very poor man's life.

In the midst of the Dallas Cowboys' surprising 2016 season, Terry appeared at my door one afternoon bearing a gift. Whenever

Terry needs my help, he brings me a gift or something of value to him so that he can barter with me.

"Man, look what I've found!" he exclaimed with great enthusiasm and wonder as he handed me a Dallas Cowboys cap. "Man, this cap was just layin' on the sidewalk, and I picked it up and saw it was like new. Hey, man, look at the bill. It's already fixed for you to wear." He pointed to the hat, the bill not curled on either side, but folded up across the entire bill and toward the crown of the cap. "Man, put that on backwards and you got it like you need it! It even matches that jacket you got on! Larry, I want you to have it."

Joy abounds, and so often, it is connected to trouble and difficulty. But it always prevails and surprises and satisfies and infects and deepens connections and builds bridges. On that special day, the "day of the Cowboys cap," we laughed so hard and made such a scene that those around us took note and joined us in the joy that has become a common experience for me, as well as almost always a prerequisite for personal and community breakthroughs. And, in that regard, it's been extremely satisfying to see Terry find an apartment and move off the streets of Dallas.

Dr. Jeff Zsohar, our medical partner in our community health improvement efforts, once told me, "I find my joy in caring for the people who live in the Cottages"—the community of fifty of the most challenging formerly homeless residents in any of our housing efforts. We are accustomed to the outcroppings of joy in our work. It is just how joy works.

Recognize That People Can't Avoid Much Evil or Do Much Good without Money

Sorry, it's just true. Joy always transcends material categories. And, as a result, it connects easily to the forces of joy working for justice. And justice involves concern for the fair distribution of wealth. People cannot live without material provisions. While money and economic power are not sources of joy, access to reasonable resources for life results in thankfulness and joy among attentive people.

At the same time, blaming people who are poor for some of the things they do is patently unfair.

How many of us experience the need for restroom facilities during the normal course of every day? If you said 100 percent of us, you would be correct. How many extremely poor people who have no home find themselves in need of restroom facilities on a daily basis? Again, if you said 100 percent, you would be correct. Yet every day, homeless people, many of whom are my friends, get in trouble with merchants, property owners, and law enforcement officials simply because they need a restroom and can't find access to one.

By definition, a penniless person suffers deeply.

Joy is hard to unlock if you have nothing but yourself and your common life problems. Joy often arrives in a folded green bank note. In the moment of tormenting need, and with no assets in hand, it is just that simple. We always drive for longer term solutions, and in these efforts joy emerges. But we must not rush to the expectation of joy if we remain unwilling to provide the basics for every person in our communities.

Without income, even the possibility of joy retreats to a distant horizon like a disappointing mirage. To entice joy, embrace realism when it comes to poverty. Put the need for capital in its proper place. Imagine how your life would be and where joy could be discovered if you were flat broke all the time. Often, joy emerges in just the right way when everyone finds enough to live on in the midst of understanding friends.

Your Turn

1. Why are we so hard on extremely poor people who ask us for help when money is involved? How does a panhandler make you feel? What thoughts do you have regarding the very poor?
2. Recount an incident of authentic joy in your life experience. What made it so joyous? Was it sustained or not? Why?
3. How does joy relate to work for justice in your mind and experience? Explain your feelings.
4. What has been your most satisfying experience of a community? Explain and reflect.
5. How can joy be planted at work? Or can it?

NOTE

[1]"The Better Teacher," Unknown source—appeared on *Church of the Savior* daily blog: http://inwardoutward.org/2016/11/03/the-better-teacher/.

CHAPTER ELEVEN

KEEP THE BACK DOOR OPEN

Working in partnerships always seems to get tedious.

Working in teams inside your own shop presents challenges that can test continuing diligence, to say nothing of challenging team chemistry. Group assignments and working arrangements are essential to progress, but sometimes such connections present project-threatening meltdowns because of differences of perspective, opinion, backgrounds, and previous life experiences.

Without great effort, coaching attention, and real commitment, teams and partnerships tend naturally to unravel.

At worst, teams can blow up. Or, on second thought, just fall apart, which can be worst of all. People leave because of disagreements, personality conflicts, better offers, and time constraints.

It is also true that across the life of such connections, people choose to come and go from collective impact efforts. It's just reality. And at times, the movement in and out and back and forth can be useful.

My point here is simple and pragmatic. Smart organizations and savvy leaders "keep the back door open" for the late arrival, premature departure, and subsequent return of partners, team members, and other participants in the work they seek to accomplish together. Leaving a project or a group should not necessarily mean that one cannot return. The function of the open back door demonstrates its real value over time. When I am secure enough to give others the grace to simply "do what they can," the payoff can be significant.

People Who Depart

Most people multitask simply because they have so much going on! Workloads ebb and flow. Priorities shift. Capacity to honor commitments is seldom completely open ended. What seemed positive and possible at the beginning for me may, over an extended period of time, evolve into a burden or drop down several notches on my priority work plan. Especially in collaborative efforts and partnerships, there may come a time for renegotiating roles and expectations. My partners and I may disagree. Rather than create a negative energy drain over a dispute, I may look for a way to graciously bow out in as inconspicuous a manner as possible. I may need to leave a group for any number of reasons. And I should understand and support others who feel the same need. On numerous occasions, I've had to bow out of groups simply because of time constraints and other mounting obligations over which I found I had no control.

There are many reasons why people leave collaborations.

Provide exit ramps with easy access.

Let people leave.

It will be okay!

People Who Return

One reason why this is true and smart is the simple fact that, just as people will leave collective efforts, people often return.

Flexibility may return to schedules. Priorities shift. People discover that a previous involvement in work with your group provided more impact, results, and satisfaction than could be recognized until they took some time away. Love for the mission sometimes overcomes whatever dispute, previous judgment, or personal constraint led to departure. When people leave and then desire to return, all things being equal, smart leaders provide for a gracious welcome back. Yes, grace can be an extremely practical tool for building group effectiveness.

And why not? In so many cases, to deny or to block the return of a valued colleague is short-sighted, petty, and unwise. Often, people who come back to a group or a project return with new enthusiasm, insight, and vigor. This is especially the case if the return is as painless as possible. Every situation is unique for sure. But in general, leaders who get things done welcome gifted players back into the game, taking time to celebrate their return and open the door for reentry, feedback, and reflection regarding the reason and timing for the return.

Test Case: Community Collaboration

As I've already mentioned, several years ago, my organization received an invitation from a local, revered family foundation to join a group of community collaborators to develop specialized housing for a group of the hardest-to-house homeless people living in Dallas. As we began, the group's key partners included representatives from the local association responsible for executing the federal government's plan to end homelessness in communities like Dallas; our housing development arm; the local mental health services provider for homeless people; the city's homeless services center; Dallas County's criminal justice department; an outside group facilitator and expert on homelessness and permanent supportive housing; a public relations firm employed by the foundation;

representatives from the University of Texas Southwestern Medical School interested in measuring outcomes and the impact of the project on the lives of those who would eventually live in the new community; the social services sector, which included my organization and another well-known local group; the mental health coverage provider; the City of Dallas; the architectural firm chosen for the design work; and the Dallas Housing Authority.

The project took over seven years to design, fund, build, and occupy. The project drove us all crazy! We completed it, and it has been a great success, attracting interest from all over the world.

As I reflect on our effort, the group dynamics interest me most about the entire process. Over the course of the long project, our group met an average of twice a month, and in the early going, more often. Some people joined our effort understanding that they would play a role, make their contribution, and then depart having accomplished their comparatively narrow mission for the effort. Others reached the point where the frustration level and the specter of only wasted time just got to be too much. They had to leave. For some of this group, they had to take a break. Some left because they moved out of the city, and in one case, out of the country!

Understandably, we had some tension in our group. The development target with its specialized population kept moving on us. Some group members wondered if everyone was being honest and transparent. Members concerned about community impact expressed other deep concerns. The public relations folks feared a media meltdown at times! Near the end, a group within the group informed us that they were done. The money was too hard to raise. The details too complex to count on. The risk not worth the potential professional and political blowback. Some of us were just tired. The group shrank. But those who remained kept working.

Throughout the life of the entire project, down to the premature grand opening, the group, in one expression or another, never quit.

People left.

People returned.

New people joined.

We welcomed people.

We sent people off into other places of responsibility.

The point is the group process remained continually dynamic from start to finish.

We allowed each other to be real, to be friends, to be professional, and, most of all, to be okay.

We kept the back door open from the first day. And, frankly, that door remains open for people to come and to go even now as we track outcomes and manage the challenging project day to day.

Donors and Politicians

Now, a word on behalf of our sponsors!

Not much gets done without involving investors, often referred to as donors. I prefer the word "investor" because of what it implies about the people and organizations that receive funding from those with money to give. The fine art of philanthropy and the wonderful work of philanthropists depend on organizations with the intelligence and know-how to get significant things done in communities for people. When donors see themselves as investors in our work, the potential for long-term relationships becomes self-evident. Of course, putting together an investment campaign or group that functions like a venture capital endeavor depends on your ability to measure and report on the work your investors underwrite. More and more, donors see themselves as investors with a mission and objective in mind, and they intend to see good work accomplished that delivers on the "initial public offering" of your project or endeavor. Seldom will you receive funds these days without the attendant requirement to demonstrate with data and qualitative narratives the impact and the success of your work, past and future. Community change and improvement are your return on investment.

In a world like this, investors come and go. A few donors will appear fickle, and some are fickle indeed. Most will invest for a time and then move on to other ventures. Ironically, sometimes that will be the result of your success, a most frustrating reality! At times, the departure of an investor should be understood as a vote of confidence in the work and performance of your programs and your team. For others, new projects, whether start-ups or targeted, high-impact opportunities, will divert some of your donors elsewhere. The fact that funding is tied to the stock market or to social pressure from friends and competing institutions means that it will always ebb and flow. It is just part of the sector's tough reality.

Always keep the back door open to investors. When you first engaged with donors, you likely welcomed them at the front door with proper introductions and full credits in media of all sorts. The arrival of donors is always encouraging news. But, as I say, donors leave, most often with no fanfare and out the back door. When donors leave, do all you can to express your gratitude and include a "final" (but not your last word to them!) report and expression of thanks. Make it clear that you hope to welcome them back at some point. Try to schedule an exit interview to get candid feedback on the decision to leave your work as an investor. Keep that information handy. Look for ways to get these donors back. That back door may become the donor's chosen path of reentry to your work.

Years ago, a good friend and professional colleague made a year-end donation to our, at that time, small organization. His gift of $40,000 allowed us to expand vital programming, and it came out of nowhere, unsolicited. At the time of the first gift, he told me that I could expect it annually until further notice. What a timely and important investment for us. In the fourth year, the gift did not arrive as normal. And I had not heard from the donor for a while—likely an error on my part for not staying more connected to such an important investor. When I called, he apologized profusely. He expressed regret as he informed me that the funds available were being shifted to another endeavor in which he now served in a leadership position. He decided to shift his investment funding.

His "mistake" was in not informing me. In fact, donors don't make mistakes; they make decisions. I remember being disappointed and, yes, a little angry and frustrated—until I thought it through. I had failed to bring him into our world to let him see the impact we were having on people trapped in deep poverty. It was all "my bad."

One thing I determined to do in response over the next several years was to treat him as I should have before he redirected his funding. And I checked to make sure that our back door stood wide open for him. Recently, my friend called me to inform me that he was about to make a significant investment in our organization again. As before, this donor wanted to engage in a strategic decision to help us move toward even more effective work in the city. With donors who want to invest, the open back door symbolizes the opportunity to do just that.

Political leaders represent a special group of investors. They expect even more in the way of reporting on outcomes and the delivery of services. In addition, the required stewardship verification and audits make contracts and grants from public sources challenging, but worth the effort. We've found that moving our work to scale required public investments. We've also learned the art of working with local, state, and federal governments to accomplish the community work our representatives direct.

Politicians come and go. We don't take political positions, nor do we campaign as an organization for individual candidates or elected leaders. We do make it our business to know all our leaders from city hall to the U.S. Congress, and in some seasons, even the president and other members of the executive branch of our national government. Even more crucial, we make it our business to know the staff that usually remains in place across many administrations.

While priorities can and do change in the world of politics, we have found working with governments to be a relatively stable source of funding for the work that we do. Occasionally, changes will occur that affect our programming. If we lose a contract or fail to qualify for the next round of grant funding, we respond to our public partners with gratitude, appreciation, and, most importantly, the humility that asks them for an exit interview so that we can understand our failures and shortcomings, if there are any to address.

Again, we make sure the back door is open. And in the case of political leaders and bureaucrats, we often will welcome them back with a newfound expectation of progress. It is certainly the case that we will work with newly elected political leadership to see that the community's needs are addressed across administrations. Here in Dallas, we've had close working relationships with the city governments forming after elections for the past twenty-five years. Our leaders know they are always welcome back with gratitude. We work to gain trust so that we can operate within their world with ease and proficiency.

Locking the Back Door

There are always exceptions.

On rare occasions, someone will leave through the back door, and you'll be so relieved that you'll shut it behind him and change the locks. Occasionally, a person will depart dramatically through the front door, complete with fanfare, press, and a good bit of noise.

The chief reasons for closing that important back door relate to mission and integrity. I've encountered real wonder as I've watched the comings and goings of a dynamic group set on accomplishing something important. The lone wolf operating outside the scope and focus of an agreed-upon mission can be a significant threat. In instances like these, closing the back door protects the heart of your group.

You'll know when to shut the back door. When you do, just get up and do it.

Your Turn

1. What is the most memorable work experience you can recall that involved you working with a team of partners? Describe it.
2. Can you explain the lines of authority in the work group? Were all the members from the same group or company? Or were there representatives from more than one organization? What were the group dynamics like?
3. What makes a working group work? What makes a working group strong? Weak? Effective? Ineffective?
4. How do you feel about the "open back door" concept? Give an example from your own experience when it worked. How about when it failed or was less than ideal?
5. What qualities are needed in the leader who is committed to leaving the back door open?
6. How does the principle of the open back door relate to donors/investors from the private and the public sector in your experience? What questions do you have about these dynamics?

CHAPTER TWELVE

PAY ATTENTION TO CRITICS

Criticism.

Few of us like to hear it directed at us. In fact, most of us don't even enjoy it when leveled against another person, do we? I know that I don't like it at all. It is somewhat amusing to consider the lengths to which I often go to sidestep criticism.

I find all sorts of creative ways to justify my actions in the face of the critic. You know what I mean:

"Well, that's not what I really intended!"

"You've got to understand me here. I had no choice but to defend myself."

"The fact is no one really understands me. If they did, they wouldn't criticize me for this."

"If you were in my shoes, you'd react just like I did!"

"No way was I going to let him get away with that sort of thing!"

"If you knew all the facts, you wouldn't be so quick to criticize me."

"I saw the red light. You started yelling at me a hundred
     yards away from it!"
"I intended to pick up the office, but I just got too busy.
     Give me a break, already!"
"I did the best I could. Obviously, that's not good enough
     for you!"
"No one cares if I go ahead without asking. Why would they?"

My lists of reactions can go on and on. I become a master excuse-
maker when confronted with even an honest critic.

Sadly, at times, it doesn't stop with my rationalizing to critics
or to innocent bystanders. What comes next is even uglier. I begin
a conversation with myself! I carry on an argument internally, a
debate within my own mind and heart. Somehow, it's just important for me to establish to myself that I am not deserving of the
criticism that I've received. Often, this internal argument gives
way to external arguments with both my critics and my allies. How
easy to divide people into groups along the fault line of an honest
but negative piece of objective feedback! So, note the progression:

1. Criticism heard and "received," sort of.
2. Excuse-making and the initial explanation and
   rationalization.
3. Fuming.
4. More detailed and articulate (sometimes at least!) rationale explained.
5. Gathering allies to hear and bolster my case.
6. Development of a more comprehensive list as to why and
   how I am right and my critic or critics are wrong.
7. Shameless attempts to explain away a mistake or a failure
   or a weakness.
8. Blood pressure may rise at some point along this continuum. Or I may "stuff" all the emotions generated by my

critic so that they emerge sort of sideways at some strategic point in the future—immediate or distant, depending on my memory.

Depending on where and why this escalation of defensiveness occurs, other people may be brought into the fray. At the extreme, I create a situation where I and others expend and waste energy that could be directed toward mission and purpose, all because I don't want to honestly accept and evaluate a word of criticism from someone near me. If this repeats itself as my normal response to criticism, I can expect subpar results no matter what I tackle. Every effort worth your time and energy likely will spawn some negative reactions, evaluations, and appraisals. It's just a fact of work and of life I've had to face.

The truth is, any honest critic who is moved by a desire to see things improve is worthy of my attention.

The honest critic should be regarded as an important and necessary ally.

Critics who care about what you care about will tell you the truth almost all the time, and they should be given an honest, open hearing.

We all need the honest critic.

And I must learn to respect, appreciate, and listen to the voices and opinions of such people. Critics, rather than enemies, should be considered highly regarded assets. Any critic just "out to get you," your project, or your team should be treated with respect, given a hearing, and then dismissed. That assignment is actually manageable after a while.

Not long ago, I ran into a vociferous critic who attacked my organization, my personal philosophy concerning a central portion of our work product, and my basic motivation for championing a particular approach to a difficult but not impossible social challenge. I reached out to him, attempting to establish meaningful conversation about the issue, as well as our differences. He seemed open to a meeting, which I arranged. We met at his place of business, an interesting place. We had a long and spirited discussion. I took him a book that I had found instructive in regard to our point of contention. We talked for about an hour. I left feeling that we made progress and that, even though we still disagreed on several things, we could work together.

I was wrong. At the next large, public gathering of our work group, he stepped up his attack on our solution to the vexing problem we met to address. At that point, I simply checked him off my "helpful to engage" list.

No disrespect.

No elevated blood pressure.

No arguments or attempts to defend, justify, or persuade. He had staked out a clear position. I knew what I believed and I knew what worked in my hometown and across the nation. No reason for further argument with his gentleman.

I was kind.

I was honest.

I tried.

I respected him.

I heard his critique.

I evaluated it.

I rejected it.

There are just times when that is the best option. Notice, I did not reject the messenger. I rejected the message. And I've learned that taking a more objective approach that doesn't resort to personal attacks serves me better as I exercise leadership and champion my point of view.

If that same person raises another criticism about another subject unrelated to our first engagement, I feel it is important that I hear him out again. I have found that I take care of myself by going the extra mile and by not prejudging or stereotyping based on past experiences. Besides that, I'm looking for the truth about what works, what is effective, and what will make us all success-ful. Once a rejected critic does not mean always a rejected critic!

Don't hear me saying that this will be automatic or easy. Responding with respect to those who challenge you, especially publicly, is not an easy assignment. But taking the high road in search of objectivity is always the good road, even when you dis-cover your critic was correct. Honest openness to other points of view endears me to observers, and sometimes even to critics.

In my former life, I served as a pastor in four congregations over a span of almost twenty-five years. Along the way, I attracted a nice group of critics. Nothing all that bad, but just the normal experiences with those who found me lacking in one area or another; and believe me, there was a lot lacking to point out! Most of the critics were kind. Many wanted to help me out, and they did. Anyone who stands up every week and has to say something, whether or not they have anything to say, is a target for critics! I've made so many awful gaffs while preaching. Most are funny. Some mistakes had to be ironed out the following Sunday morning after a week of stewing on my own stupidity. After a while, I came to realize that most folks who point out the mistakes are good friends who want to see you grow and do better.

The critics with the more substantive issues are the ones who cause the heartburn and headache. These are the good people, almost all honest, who simply believe that you are wrong, pos-sibly heretical, and maybe just evil. These folks are much harder to manage because their concerns often come down to a win/lose struggle, with the loser going away. I had such a critic at my last church where I served for over fourteen years. He determined that my view of the Bible was anything but "evangelical." He regarded me as neo-orthodox and possibly downright liberal. He picked that up from my preaching, from the sources I read and studied, and from my community agenda in the church. He was so incensed that he finally wrote a personal letter to every member of the church. In the letter, he called me out for heresy, literally. He had not given me any advance notice, nor had he shared his letter with me before it showed up in my mailbox at about the same time it arrived at the home of every other member of our church. I can vividly remember crafting a letter of response to everyone in my church. The uproar necessitated the response. I remember speaking to his charges while doing my best to respect him as my critic.

I confess: the situation was difficult. I was supported by the church's leadership board. The critic and his family left the church, as did several others. It was a painful time.

Ironically, it was a time of growth as well, both personally and as a church. My critic was honest and good. He did what he felt he had to do. Somehow, I came to that conclusion rather quickly. I realized that the criticism, though its delivery rather dramatic and a real blindside, made me stronger and made our group closer and more effective. And all these years later, I'll tell you what I told those who stayed with us—in part, my critic was exactly right. I am not an "evangelical" in my approach to the Bible. Things just aren't that simple. And I'm more of a liberal than even he or I discerned at the time. By embracing the truth about myself as defined by a harsh critic, I experienced personal growth and genuine inner peace. I know I found it easier to pray! And the struggle made me stronger in faith and in perseverance.

Some situations and circumstances guarantee that criticism will arise. At one point in our housing development for homeless persons, we attempted to gain control of an old hotel property at the corner of Akard Street and I-30 on the south side of downtown Dallas. I recall attending a number of meetings with the local neighborhood association to discuss the project. We hosted a design charette. We briefed everyone on numerous occasions. We answered questions again and again. Finally, the neighbors banned together and threw us, the mayor, and the council member from the district out on our ear. Nothing personal you understand. Just not in our backyard! Not here, not now, not ever!

This one made me fighting mad—until I calmed down and realized that people often want different things. In this case, our critics were property owners. They had the support of elected officials, whom they elected and re-elected. We were defeated before we even showed up! And it wasn't our fault. We arrived well prepared, but preparation made it worse because it seemed that we might prevail. We had done our homework. In the end, we were defeated by an organized group of democracy-exploiters. The well-presented self-interests of the property owners prevailed over the pressing needs of the voiceless homeless. We had to gather up our maps, our renderings, and our big plans and hightail it back to where we came from! What a valuable lesson. Critics can be fact-tellers. They warned us. We didn't listen carefully enough. There may have been a way to win them over, but I don't think so. Our critics won. Game over. Respect maintained. We'll do battle elsewhere another day.

Ironically, years later, our housing company (CitySquare Housing) entered a partnership with a for-profit developer, helped capture the same old hotel property, and redeveloped it as a convention hotel with a mid-range, nightly price point. This time our plan worked, and we got paid for it. We put the funds earned back into our community development corporation to be used in building more affordable housing in Dallas. So our critics didn't stop us. They just diverted us toward a new, practical approach around a real opportunity. Guess who some of our loudest cheerleaders for the project are today? You guessed it, the same group that opposed our original plan. It just works this way if you take the long view on the high road, while working hard to respect your critics, no matter what. Oh, and in the process, we helped clean up a terrible corner in a key part of downtown Dallas.

One final note. Determine to be a positive, constructive critic yourself. People who are determined to get things done will take seriously the challenge of growing into the kind of critic that others appreciate and seek out. Some of your best work likely will involve you assisting allies and new friends by offering an honest, concerned word of critique in a manner in which it can be received more easily by those to whom you offer it.

Your Turn

1. Recall a time when you were the brunt of harsh criticism. Describe the situation and the details.
2. How did you feel? What were your emotions? How did you manage your emotions?
3. Did you react to your critic? How?
4. What was the aftermath of the criticism?
5. Do you have any regrets?
6. What did you take away from the experience?
7. Do you handle criticism today differently than you did in the past?
8. What is the benefit of criticism? What is its fundamental challenge?

CHAPTER THIRTEEN

WELCOME THE UNREASONABLE

The essence of innovation just may be unreasonableness.

In my own experience, I've come to realize that ideas that seem ridiculous at first glance often provide authentic breakthrough opportunities. CitySquare validates my hypothesis at virtually every turn. Again and again, we've tried what seemed like strange, new, extremely unreasonable tactics and strategies to achieve our mission. Appreciating and seriously considering unreasonable ideas serves as a fundamental value in the CitySquare Way. Consider this list of examples drawn from the life of our organization. Each represents a basic willingness to consider and to embrace what on the surface appeared beyond unreasonable, but which resulted in innovation and advancement over time.

Hiring New Workers

We turned over the day-to-day operation of our signature community outreach/engagement program to the people who used it on a regular basis as customers. We invited those who needed our food distribution initiative to run the place. And you know what? They did it! And they did it better than anyone ever had done it before them.

Redeveloping for Mixed Income

We redeveloped an abandoned fifteen-story downtown office tower into a mixed-use, mixed-income housing facility that included retail/office space and condominiums for sale at market rates. Our growth drove us to select the office building for our headquarters, and we added the notion of housing as a way to recapture the historic building, while providing great homes for low-income residents, as well as condo owners. There were so many conventional reasons not to embark on this fanciful adventure, but we ignored the common wisdom in favor of being unreasonable. This housing development delivered the first truly affordable housing to downtown Dallas in living memory. Oh, and by the way, we had virtually no cash on hand when we started the project. In fact, we closed on the complicated transaction about a month before the largest stock market crash since the Great Depression.

Distributing Food to Students in the Summer

We built a citywide food program for students who needed help with nutritious meals when our schools took a summer break. By linking the food distribution effort with AmeriCorps staffing, we delivered not just food, but a day camp experience to children who had neither where they lived. Food became a sideline to the innovation of a mobile, agile, daily youth camp right outside the students' doors every day. Were there obstacles? You bet—new liability at every turn, keeping food cold and hot, transportation of meals and staff, turf wars with groups who considered us competitors and outsiders. The list of problems and roadblocks goes on and on. But we did it because we accepted unreasonable thinking and we allowed ourselves the luxury of dreaming. We also were driven by simple recognition of the real need for what we were doing.

Housing First

As noted previously, we joined a completely unreasonable coalition to develop what is now a national best practice for homeless housing: the Cottages at Hickory Crossing. Providing high-quality "Housing First" to the most expensive and difficult homeless people in Dallas County moved us beyond unreasonable to the margins of lunacy, at least in the minds of some observers. But we did it. The residents remain grateful that someone decided to be unreasonable in face of their tough, seemingly intractable negative living situations. The Cottages work because we got downright unreasonable about homelessness.

Investing in the Future

A generous donor invested hundreds of thousands of dollars in a fund that is allowing us to buy property for future development. She has no assurances as to what we will develop. But she is willing to be creatively unreasonable with her philanthropy to advance our mission. Trust and faith provide the sinews and bones of unreasonable progress.

Trusting That the Poor Have Dreams

We trust in the unreasonable notion that poor people can accumulate real wealth once they secure employment and find the time to carefully consider their own dreams, goals, and aspirations. Our employment training programs work. I mean really work. Our unreasonable training team convinced me that those who go to work, if provided financial coaches, can be expected to save, plan, and grow their way into financial stability and health. Have you ever heard a more unreasonable idea than this: the poor can earn and grow wealth? I started as a reasonable skeptic. Today, I repent as a convert to a most unreasonable idea that works.

Watching People Change

Along these lines, another donor stepped up recently to inform us that she wanted to join us in helping low-income working people receive wealth to build and save. We continue to work with her on an extremely unreasonable new plan to do just this! We believe people can change. How unreasonable, until you watch it day after day or until you act like you believe it, even when some evidence to the contrary remains. Persisting in a fundamental belief in the capacity, the goodness, and the potential of every person we encounter is another key to progress and innovation, no matter how unreasonable it feels or sounds or appears.

More on Lowering Requirements

As noted previously, we accept the unreasonable truth about "Housing First," the housing strategy that places homeless people in housing before requiring anything else from them. No burning hoops to jump through to "earn" a home or to prove you're "housing ready." None of the typical, often moralistic prerequisites imposed on people who need a home but who present problems associated with long-term living on the street. Housing First establishes a new, extremely unreasonable platform of operations. People receive permanent housing, and then are free to choose what, if any, services they desire to receive. Submitting to program requirements that a person like me comes up with before awarding housing to a homeless person may make sense in the abstract. The fact is, however, no approach works as well as the unreasonable notion of simply placing a homeless person in a home before working on any program or any other so-called remedies.

But how do you create a culture that expects and accepts unreasonable ideas?

Well, the status quo in most organizations arrays itself against seemingly impossible challenges. Leaders must pledge to do whatever it takes to break down the forces that keep things the same and that trap people in normalcy. The key to being creatively unreasonable involves expectations of constant progress and the willingness of key people to upset the applecart of established ideas as a matter of course. Practically speaking, smart leaders seek out and hire "smart doers" and then they simply turn them loose to work out meaningful change.

Leaders and organizations that experience significant breakthroughs remain open to considering plans of action that other, more conventional decision makers would never imagine or allow to be considered. Breaking the stubborn veneer of the reasonable exemplifies the hallmark of transformative leadership.

Often, the challenges facing leaders and their organizations present themselves in highly predictable ways. Without the possibility of acting outside the norm, most of these challenges will remain unaddressed and unsolved. If we are afraid to think, plan, or act with unreasonableness, we won't see the change needed for progress. Allowing team members to fully embrace the power of being unreasonable as an essential tool in the arsenal of problem-solving will lead to brilliant, surprising breakthroughs.

What have we got to lose anyway?

So what if we try something crazy and fail? If your organization's culture leads courageously, very seldom is failure in pursuit of the unreasonable regarded as any worse than tepid support of business as usual, which produces few actual positive, life-altering results. The expectation of risking for the sake of real progress can fill an organization with hope and optimism.

After all, no one has ever changed the world without being unreasonable.

Case Study: Racial Reconciliation, Expecting the Unreasonable

Too often, bringing people together into an experience of genuine community across racial lines seems unreasonable. I mean, think about the forces at work against unity, harmony, mutual respect, open communication, and appreciation:

cultural differences
personal bias
white privilege
dearth of honest communication
systemic racism
housing policy
history
personal experiences
economic inequity
opportunity gaps
disproportionate adversity
current political climate
police brutality
fear

The list could go on.

Unreasonable Ideas

These realities, and many others, work to place the notion of racial reconciliation squarely in the unreasonable column. All the more reason to attack with full human abandon! As unreasonable as these ideas may sound, they are practical and worthwhile places to start.

Seek Out

Find a person not of your ethnic background where you work, travel, or live and begin a conversation about race and unity. Commit yourself to listening. Don't fear stupid questions. The fact that you are willing to ask and seek to understand will elevate the conversation to a surprising level where amazing things can happen. Don't be defensive. Be respectful in conversation, even if you feel misunderstood, judged, or rejected. Be honest about your own feelings and experiences. Don't allow your conversation to be a one-and-done deal. Seek to establish an ongoing conversation with your new found understanding partner. When it makes sense, work with your partner to expand the conversation to others in your world.

If you are an employer or the boss, allow your newfound understandings to inform your hiring decisions. You won't regret these steps. I tell our team all the time that we cannot afford to "bleach" our team with easy, but ill-advised hiring practices. Improvement follows intentionality. Intentionality in chasing this unreasonable idea pays rich dividends.

Visit

Visit a faith community not of your ethnic or racial background. A familiar assessment of Sunday mornings in this country that I'm sure you've heard goes something like this: "Sunday morning remains the most segregated hour of the week." That may be true in some sense, though I expect it doesn't take into account just how many hours a week are virtually completely segregated in our neighborhoods and in our public schools. Public education is more segregated today, especially in the urban centers, than it was forty years ago. Still, a great experience can be found in sharing worship with others not of your ethnicity. Worship style, liturgical variety, interpretive background and history, expectation, and purpose surrounding the worshipping community will open doorways to even deeper understanding of those who don't share the same racial background and heritage. Being intentional about choosing intersections between yourself and others unlike you racially will pay rich results.

For eleven years, my wife and I were members of an African American church in Dallas. We chose to make this connection. It was a fascinating, deliberate journey we took. It opened us up to a new world of beautiful people. It would be impossible for me to attach a proper value to the experience. Words like rich, wonderful, surprising, educational, humbling, loving, vulnerable, fun, funny, inexhaustible, long, and fulfilling come to mind as I try to describe our experience. For some people who watched us in this experience, I know we seemed unreasonable. And maybe we were. However, what started out as a seemingly unreasonable choice ended up being among the most reasonable decisions we've ever made, and one that paid rich dividends for everyone involved.

Move

Decide to live in a racially mixed neighborhood. Sound unreasonable? For many of us, it will. Those who move into fully integrated communities will find such a move marvelously reasonable after they've been settled in for a while.

This brings me back to the segregated nature of our public schools. In Dallas, most neighborhoods remain pretty much segregated. What is different about today's segregation has to do with economic status. While poverty in urban centers disproportionately affects people of color, the economic diversity drives and defines today's experience of segregation. Poor people are also people of color. As a result, chances are moving into a racially mixed community also means you will be moving into a poorer neighborhood.

Go for it!

I love what I observe among young couples making conscious, principled decisions to stay with the public schools all the way to their children's graduations. The benefit and value of the experience of education in a context of cultural and ethnic diversity can't be accurately estimated. All I know is that out of seemingly unreasonable decisions like this, great benefit flows in every direction.

My experience tells me that attacking the unreasonable challenge of achieving racial reconciliation will involve us in the forces of presence, proximity, purpose, passion, persistence, and performance. It can be done, no matter how unreasonable it may sound.

Your Turn

1. Think of something unreasonable that you've done at some point in your life. Tell the story of your flight of fancy.
2. How did things work out for you as you acted in this manner? Negatives? Positives?
3. What unreasonable actions are you considering or currently involved in now? How's it going for you?
4. When you pursue unreasonable ideas or actions, how does it make you feel?
5. How unreasonable is the notion of racial reconciliation in your community today? Explain your answers.

CHAPTER FOURTEEN

GIVE AWAY
WHAT YOU NEED

Summer 1995, or thereabouts, I witnessed something beyond precious. As I recall, we faced a typical Texas scorcher of a day. Around the edges of our food pantry and upstairs for some relief from the heat, we operated a summer camp for children. The children involved in the camp experience moved back and forth from outside to inside. Children not involved with the camp stuck close to parents who came for food assistance from our little food pantry. The image I can still see involved two small boys, one about two or three years older than his younger brother, who sat close by his side, taking in the chaos of our operations. Somehow, the older brother managed to get a banana. I watched with interest as he carefully peeled the piece of fruit and divided it cleanly and exactly in half. He handed his younger sibling half, and watched as his brother scarfed down the treat. He then ate his own portion of the small meal.

I knew both were hungry.

I knew the older brother would have enjoyed the whole banana and likely needed it. But he had to care for his brother. That's just how they rolled.

That scene, which I can still remember vividly, touched me deeply and reflected a kind of giving in the midst of real life that transforms people and spotlights larger purpose. In many ways, this story remains too sacred to be used to illustrate a pragmatic reality.

But, then again, maybe not.

To get things done, you must learn to give away exactly what you need most in order to fulfill your purpose and to do your work. When you give away what you obviously need yourself, people will notice and doors will open to productive action.

Time

Everyone needs all the time they can get, save, and utilize. All of us press to figure out how to manage time, bank time, extend time, and use time as effectively as possible. When you give time away, it is your life you are transferring to another person or organization. I expect this is why most of us hate interruptions. We make our plans. We allocate our minutes and our days. Interruptions can feel like highway robbery! And on many occasions, this assessment is spot on. But not always.

Giving time to another person usually turns out to be a positive decision. When such gifting or sacrifice occurs on a team between team members and/or leaders, the impact can be immeasurably positive. Leaving the door unlocked and positioned slightly open to others in your world can allow for investments in the lives and efforts of teammates, family members, customers, friends, and even perfect strangers.

The locked door may also serve an important purpose at times. Pablo Picasso once noted that "without great solitude no serious work is possible."[1] So we must admit the importance of working without interruption when necessary. But we need balance and to develop an appreciation for the power of giving time to others.

An important discipline, when it comes to giving away your time, will be reframing. Most of the time when people break into what I am doing in order to snatch away some of this precious commodity, I have to fight back feelings of resentment. Just recalibrating from one important activity to an interruption takes energy on my part, and at times, I must admit, it aggravates me!

But I'm learning to reframe my aggravation in such a way that I can regard interruptions as opportunities to invest some of the treasure of my life in other people and their projects and priorities. Few things will endear you as deeply or as quickly as your willingness to give up and give away your time for the sake of another person. Talk about boosting morale, bolstering loyalty, and building a team. When you give away your time, you make an investment that will pay off richly over time.

Being available as a leader is absolutely essential to your success. We all need time. When we give it away with purpose and intentionality, we take important steps toward achieving our goals. Investing time in the lives of others enhances their abilities and multiplies their chances of being successful. Such investments also inspire loyalty while renewing devotion to your overall mission.

In regard to time, if you make an impact in your work, you may expect to be approached by others who seek to glean wisdom and knowledge from your experiences. I almost never turn away those who seek to learn from our successes and our failures. In the long run, sharing time, advice, stories, and joys never diminishes me. Rather, I am made stronger by surrendering my time to honest seekers. Over the years, we've assisted many groups in attaining their own nonprofit status, and we've never been made poorer for sharing the gift of time with its accompanying talent, experience, learning, and attention offered to others, and offered freely and gladly.

Treasure

Now, I move to meddling.

Leaders who seek what's best for their teams and their communities will give away funds to other leaders and organizations for the larger good of the whole in which they work.

This one is tough! We all need funding. We work hard at getting funded. Frankly, we often approach seeking funding as a competitive sport or, worse still, a battle. After all, if my organization is to thrive and survive, I must secure the funding I need to continue my work, right? So why would I ever entertain the thought of helping someone else or some other group secure the same funding that I need from a limited pool of resources available in my community or donor pool?

I won't, if I am typical.

But isn't it good to remember that great dreams and accomplishments don't usually traffic in the typical?

Genuine concern for the good of the community, the sector, and the overall progression of our values and our commitments calls for an open-handed approach to funding efforts and to our neighbors and colleagues. Still, this can get tough fast in the real world.

Not long ago, I met with a local foundation as part of their grant-making process. We had submitted a proposal seeking a large gift, the largest we had ever sought from this particular source. I arrived for my meeting a bit early and just in time to encounter a nonprofit leader from another organization that I admire a great deal. Clearly, he was after some of the same funding that I sought. His organization does amazing work using legal tools and options to identify and shut down crack houses in an impoverished part of our city. His work represents the best in innovation, progress, measurable objectives, and integrity. This organization, under my friend's capable leadership, accomplishes some of the most important work in our community.

One of the leaders of this particular foundation fund has been a friend for decades, as my family knew his family for a long time. I felt positive about our prospects of being funded. When I saw the other nonprofit executive, I realized that I had a responsibility to speak the truth to the foundation board. So my first words were to endorse the efforts of his group and to urge the foundation to help him out. It was the right and obvious thing to do. And I'm confident that my show of support helped my friend with the foundation.

I also am convinced it helped us.

The willingness to give up for others for the good of the whole is a principle I've embraced for a long time. Sometimes, your decisions along these lines are observed by others, as in this case. Most times, no one knows or sees as you pursue the higher ground of giving up treasure for a larger good beyond your own immediate self-interest. None of this is about me. It is about the culture of our organization and the values we have embraced intentionally. Over and over again, the results have been more than gratifying. Become accustomed to giving away what you feel you need. Again and again, we've connected people and groups outside our organization for their good and not ours. From an IT training company to a start-up specialty food company to countless nonprofits and aspiring nonprofit organizations, we have learned that there is great benefit in being open to helping others along toward their own successes. Investing the treasure you have or that which you seek in others will reap a rich dividend in the end.

We have "competitors" as resident tenants on our properties. We support them in their funding and community relationship building simply because it is what we do. Even more, it is who we are.

Your Turn

1. Think of a time when you gave something away that you needed. Describe how it felt to give away something that you needed yourself.
2. How can you reframe the interruptions caused by eager people seeking your time, wisdom, and advice?
3. What have you gained from giving yourself away or giving away what you needed?
4. Can you make a difference by having a larger focus than your own needs or those of your organization? How?
5. Are you open to the notion of leading with "open handedness"?

NOTE

[1]Inward/Outward, a project of Church of the Saviour in Washington, DC, "Serious Work," Washington, DC, January 11, 2017, http://inwardoutward.org /2017/01/11/serious-work/.

CHAPTER FIFTEEN

LEAD FLAT

From a traditional understanding and experience of power and leadership, the idea that effective leaders work hard to press decision-making downward as deep into their organizations as possible may sound and even feel strange. Nothing could be further from the truth today. Leaders must be distributed throughout organizations that expect to endure, sustain, and experience ongoing renewal while driving innovation. Effective teams will expect to find leaders from the line staff to the C suites who are equipped to deliver direction and vision for responsive team members. In fact, truly successful organizations expect leadership to emerge from diverse places, roles, and positions of responsibilities throughout the organization.

It is from this expectation of leadership discovery throughout an entire team that leaders can begin to involve every team member in decision-making and in the debate and open dialogue that should be taking place as decisions are made. Often, the more important the decision, the flatter the team leadership is and the more involved visionary leaders become across the larger group.

Hierarchy doesn't get it done like it once did. And today, I wonder if it ever did. While there will come times when someone must make ultimate decisions, in almost every instance, the engagement of leadership ideas, insights, and perspectives from the entire team will prove essential in arriving at the best determination regarding opportunities, challenges, and overcoming barriers.

A top-down leadership style limits your ability to penetrate challenges because it typically leaves assets on the table that remain unused, untouched, and unrecognized—key assets that could have been essential to important breakthroughs and success.

Top-down leadership limits the leader's power because it truncates buy-in. Sadly, in all too many places, leaders who dictate from above and team members who work busily below never think about or imagine new, different, or innovative ways of getting things done. Organizations that are not open to ideas "from below" with leaders arrayed only above consign themselves to mediocrity and the dull, dull world of business as usual.

But how does an organization set the culture for pervasive, expansive, organization-wide leadership that can be called upon and, in fact, expects to be called upon for creative thinking and effective decision-making? How does the expectation of leading flat by reaching out to a larger team of leaders with authenticity, courage, and honesty emerge in an organization or group? Clearly, organizational development along the lines of leading flat only results when we plan and act intentionally.

Consider three essentials for building a flat leadership team.

First, build a solid team on its way to greatness. We quote Jim Collins a lot around my shop. One of his most important values and possibly our favorite Collins idea about team building involves "getting the right people on the bus."[1] It was often said of iconic Dallas Cowboys coach Tom Landry that he always drafted for talent and not position. So it is in building a team filled with leaders up and down the roster.

Hire smart to lead flat. Staffing decisions will make or break you in this endeavor. The development of human resources is essential to growing the culture required to produce a broad array of leaders who touch and represent every part of your enterprise. Not long ago, we received notice from the mayor's office concerning an important meeting that would focus and coordinate efforts in one particularly tough part of the city. From relevant email messages, it did not appear that crucial members of our team would be attending the meeting. I got involved by sending an alert to two key leaders to determine if they would attend the meeting. They replied that they were both already committed to other activities. So, I decided to go and represent us. When I arrived and stepped into the meeting room, I was greeted by four of our program staff whose area would be affected by any decisions made at the meeting. They were way ahead of me. They were fully informed about the meeting, and they were ready to go to work! These committed leaders were way ahead of "the boss." The leaders closest to the opportunity acted on the possibility to see things improve. I excused myself, noting that the experts were already in the house, and went on to my next appointment, thanks to these highly capable leaders.

Second, create vested interests among both your leadership team and your entire organization to the end that everyone feels as if they have a personal stake in team success. This requires genuine buy-in on the part of leaders. You must communicate that responsibility, for success extends from top to bottom and from side to side throughout your team. Your mission must be compelling, even world-changing, especially in the nonprofit sector where personal financial success usually is not the target. This reminds me of the possibly apocryphal story of a custodian working at NASA during the lunar exploration campaign inspired by President John F. Kennedy. When asked what his job was, the janitor replied proudly, "I'm putting a man on the moon!" This is what we're looking to replicate in our organization.

Third, recognize the importance of alignment when it comes to building great teams full of trustworthy leaders. Identifying talent that can be intentionally coupled with others in complementary ways results in strong action units. These units can be depended upon with the expectation of great accomplishments. When teams of people share common objectives, are led by those authorized to act out of their own leadership skill, and are deployed against any challenge defined by the group's mission, the chances of success rise exponentially.

Years ago, when we were a much, much smaller organization, we set up a staff meeting process that challenged top-down, hierarchical thinking. Rather than me, as the leader and planner of the meeting, bringing a predetermined agenda to work through, I began our time together by asking everyone in the group to help us "build our agenda" for the meeting. The first several times we structured our meetings like this, people seemed reluctant to participate. Clearly, they felt caught off guard. However, once accustomed to the process, the group responded positively and we enjoyed more engaging meetings. At one point, a new team member joined us from another organization. He chided me for "abdicating my leadership" by allowing the staff to enjoy such power and influence on our organizational strategy and tactics. I explained that the new input process always managed to cover the essentials, provided me with new insight about what everyone felt were the essentials, and, in fact, did not deviate far from the agenda I would bring to each meeting. I'm not sure I ever convinced him of the benefit of my loose hand on the reins! While he insisted on a more controlling approach, engaging every team member as a leader and a partner in defining our group agenda communicated a great deal about just how much I trusted my team.

Without authentic trust in your team and in the individuals that form it, leading flat will prove impossible. Leaders who communicate their faith in their teams will enjoy great success as everyone finds their place while feeling liberated to inform the group's larger work. The challenge for leaders who don't appreciate flat leadership will be centered around predictable issues associated with control, power, credit, and failure. The payoff from pressing leadership deep into your group will become evident fairly quickly when those you lead understand that you are serious about trusting them to lead in their places of responsibility no matter where they fall on the organization chart.

Your Turn

1. What do you think about this notion of leading flat? What are the challenges?
2. What are the challenges to top-down leadership strategies? How did you react to the agenda-setting strategy?
3. What do you feel is necessary to equip and prepare an organization for a flat leadership style?
4. How challenging do you feel it will be to train team members to exercise leadership no matter where they serve in your organization? What will be required where you work and serve today?
5. If you were drafting team members, would you focus on the specific position need of your organization or would you focus on finding the best player? Explain.
6. Was the janitor really putting a man on the moon? Justify your answer.

NOTE

[1]Jim Collins, *Good to Great: Why Some Companies Make the Leap . . . and Others Don't* (New York: HarperCollins, 2001), 41.

CHAPTER SIXTEEN

IMAGINE PARTNERS

Complex problems cry out for partnerships. Reducing poverty cannot be accomplished by a single organization or singular approach. What is true for poverty and pathways out of its cruel clutches is true for other daunting problems and challenges. Nothing significant can be achieved without trusted partners who sign on to link arms and move into the challenging fray together. Wise leaders spend a good bit of time thinking about connecting with others to form effective partnerships. Imagining what kind of partners and partnerships might advance your cause and the causes of any potential partners is a great way to spend your dream time. Solid partners make a huge difference. And partnerships can take all sorts of shapes and styles.

Partnership One: Improvement through Cooperation

We've been at work in the community health-care space since 1990, serving the medical needs of uninsured, inner city residents of East and South Dallas. For years, we attempted, with varying degrees of success, to provide dental services as well. But we weren't very good at it. Keeping dentists engaged and bearing with demanding patients (from the dentists' points of view!), as well as our inability to perform "deep dentistry," including root canals and implants, and the rising cost of our services all conspired to paralyze us. Rather quickly, we solved all our problems related to dental services through a creative partnership orchestrated by another partner—sort of a partner intervening with another partner to solve our problem. For years, the Agape Clinic located at Grace United Methodist Church had been a "competitor" in the healthcare field. Calling them a competitor may sound strange, but take it from me, it is honest. Thanks to another partner, Highland Park United Methodist Church, that provided essential funding, we contracted with Agape to do all our dental work. Agape built its capacity dramatically thanks to their partnership with Texas A&M University and Baylor University School of Dentistry, itself an amazing partnership. Agape built a state-of-the-art dental clinic thanks to Highland Park UMC. This circle of innovative cooperation goes on and on! The bottom line: our neighbors receive high-quality dental services like never before. The lines of the partnership weave a web of healing and care like none of us could ever have provided alone. Submitting to the leadership of others, while receiving huge benefit as an organization and as a recruiter of patients, has been a wonderfully humbling experience, one that we all needed, especially me. Most of the problems we face are much bigger and call for solutions much more complicated and comprehensive than we can realistically expect to handle alone.

Partnership Two: Practical Engagement

In the spring of 2016, a huge "tent city" sprang up under one of I-45's overpass bridges. When the City of Dallas provided portable toilets and trash dumpsters, the community grew to well over three hundred people. The result: an unstable, unsafe, unhealthy environment not fit for human habitation. The city moved decisively to shut it down. The drama grew quickly. We had people vowing to stay no matter what. We had a preacher and his wife chain themselves to one of the concrete support columns under the bridge and threaten not to leave until everyone found housing! The tension mounted as the days and weeks passed along. After about two months, and with a great deal of warning, the city removed the tents and all the occupants. Metro Dallas Homeless Alliance (MDHA) led the way in organizing the removal of the tent city. We were asked to join in the effort, along with a couple of other groups. The whole situation presented one heartbreaking situation after another. The good news was that we found permanent housing for almost one hundred people in an intense, ninety-day effort.

The folks we removed had organized a city, complete with a town council and a mayor! Mike Rawlings, the mayor of Dallas, met with the tent city mayor to discuss solutions. Tent owners organized their community into blocks and lots, complete with berms and boundaries clearly marked into streets and lanes, all because the community found ways to get organized around toilets and trash containers. We entered the partnership quietly, simply, and with clear determination to house people who lived in tents. We eagerly submitted to leadership from MDHA and the City of Dallas. A clean, clear partnership allowed us to do good work with equally hard-working partners. In the aftermath of that effort, we found it easier to follow "the swirl" of people created every time an encampment closed down, and several more were closed and their residents removed. Heartache gave way to grim resolve to work together to get people into housing. As sad as our work turned out to be, we felt renewed by our connection and thankful for our partners.

Partnership Three: Day-to-Day Environment

In November 2014, we opened the Opportunity Center on Malcolm X Boulevard at the gateway to historic South Dallas/Fair Park. We designed and constructed the 54,000-square-foot campus to function as a collective impact center. The business rationale behind the development included our commitment to seek rent-paying tenants who would join in an effort to create a one-stop shop of options and services for neighbors seeking to move up and out of poverty to better lives.

It worked. Literacy Instruction for Texas (LIFT), the best literacy, GED prep, and ESL instructors in the city; Workforce Solutions Greater Dallas (the Texas WorkForce Commission in Dallas County and beyond); Per Scholas, an IT training company out of the Bronx in New York City; numerous local, grassroots community groups; and CitySquare all occupy the campus for the good of the city. The collective defines itself as a grand partnership on steroids! Hundreds of people seeking better options for themselves and their families visit the campus every day. I don't know why it took us so long to take this important step forward. For certain, no one wants to go backward into isolation.

Building Partnerships

So how do you build effective partnerships? This is an essential question for leaders to ponder. Finding the correct answers can be determinative for the effectiveness and success of your organization. Consider the following essentials for constructing partnerships.

Focus on Trust and Build It

Nothing will be more important to you and your partners as you move forward than certainty about your dependability and commitment, not only regarding the work you share but also the personal relationships you build, protect, and count on. Every great partnership I've enjoyed over the years has been built over time on a solid foundation of trust.

We have to be realistic about trust building. Forming trusted connections takes time. I need to understand that building a lasting, productive relationship with a partner necessitates lots of meetings, conversations, debates, and some settings for social interaction. Almost without exception, my best partnerships across the years involved people and organizations that I grew to call friends and allies. Again, partners must be able to trust one another. If that is possible, you have the raw ingredients for productive action. Trust creates the atmosphere that makes alignment of resources, interests, missions, and even mid-course corrections possible. Trust includes having your partner's back. Trust means that credit will be shared freely, so freely that seeing a partner receive thanks and expressions of appreciation for work well done is every bit as satisfying, and maybe even more satisfying, as receiving thanks yourself (see Chapter Five). Trust means that partners never throw one another under an out-of-control bus on which they may be riding! Trust provides the foundation needed to sustain connections, enhance the quality of the work you do, and move forward with a purpose and an effectiveness you could not expect to achieve on your own. Trust is so essential to partnerships that it is almost always worth whatever wait is necessary for its development and maturation. Trust is the glue that holds partners together over the long haul. Without trust, no real partnership can grow or endure.

Communicate; Talk Again and Again

I'm not a fan of the cell phone. Still, I use it every day, all day long and into the night. I'm aggravated by the emails that fill my inbox every morning and through the night. But, I must admit, I'm not sure how I would function without it. I hate meetings, but my life is one long, unending meeting, or so it seems at times. Taken together, all of these sometimes frustrating realities of my life function as indispensable tools I must use in building effective partnerships.

Why? Communication is essential to the process of constructing partnerships. While I complain about the tools and the way in which they chain me to work, I find my work satisfying because I love people and I enjoy communicating. No worthwhile partnership will ever become a routine part of your work and life without regular communication with your potential or current partners. In fact, without communication—regular, planned, intentional communication—no partnership can survive, let alone thrive. The more you can communicate with partners, the more effective you will become. If communication dries up, get ready for failure and disappointment. Communication is so important to sustaining effective partnerships that one of the most important actions you can take as you plan your daily routine is to build in time for communicating with key partners. When it comes to communication, intentional action serves mission.

Test the Culture and the Values of Potential Partners

As you go about the essential work of building trust and focusing on committed communication, keep your eyes and ears open to what you hear and observe from the world of any potential partner. If your values don't line up with those of prospective partners, back away. Partnerships are too time consuming and important to engage another organization whose values and culture turn out to be incompatible with yours. Organizations should be complementary from a work-product standpoint so that each can deliver various dimensions of what's necessary to adequately address a challenge. While work focus and specialties should vary in most cases, with various partners bringing their unique and essential expertise to the partnership table, partner values should form one strong backbone that all agree upon. If values do not line up consistently, the outcomes almost always turn out less than optimal. I've been fortunate in my work experience to mostly avoid what I call a "value mismatch." The few examples that do come to mind from my experience are anything but pleasant. Be careful with whom you decide to team up.

Operate as a Deal Maker

By that I mean work to serve your vision and that of your partnership. If the vision is legitimate, no effort is too big. Partnerships almost always link back to some leader whose thinking falls into the category of bringing forces, resources, people, and options together in surprising new ways. The dealmaker resembles an artist at work on a fresh canvas. She invites others to join in the creative work, but she never forgets the canvas and how the various images come together or can come together with the correct palette, brush, and careful hand. Dealmakers allow ideas to remain open-ended and free form, especially during the incubation period. These special, visionary leaders give big ideas the freedom and the space they need to form, morph, evolve, and grow. The leader I have in mind functions as a craftsman who knows when to back away to give a great idea the freedom to become too big, too significant to fail. Dealmakers find ways to create highly effective partnerships. It is just what they do.

You'll know when you face a partnership opportunity. One clear marker will be your move from monthly brown bag lunch meetings in which people gather up all their stuff at meeting's end, leaving nothing of value on the table, to meetings where real assets are placed on the table and left there as investments in the partnership's effort.

Your Turn

1. Think about a time you worked in a highly successful partnership. Describe what made it work.
2. Now, consider a less than successful partnership. What contributed to its failure?
3. Why is trust so important in partnerships?
4. Have you ever been in a partnership or a connection where values were not aligned? Describe that experience.
5. How do you feel when you think of yourself as a dealmaker? Why?
6. Are partnerships essential in achieving most worthy objectives? Explain your feelings.

CULTIVATE CHAOS

It is a hard truth: nothing changes or improves that remains unshaken. Leaders who get things done shake things up. Disruption is a fine art, a balancing act that most always ought to be intentional and strategic. One of our core principles at CitySquare is the fact that we value chaos and ownership. Ownership, because if people don't fully embrace or buy in to our ideas or efforts, we will not be effective or successful. Chaos, because we seek to leave plenty of room for faith and trust to work out in our mission.

Years ago, I enjoyed an amazing and unique opportunity that lasted for a little over fourteen years. The church where I grew up called me home to serve as its senior minister. As I planned my work, I settled on a clear and focused strategy for myself and the church, a strategy that I kept largely to myself. Especially in the beginning, I just acted on my internal vision. First, I resolved to lead the church in pursuit of a thoroughly ecumenical agenda. Our tradition began as an ecumenical movement, but lost its way over generations before falling off into a rigid, paralyzing legalism. I was convinced that the way to health and growth would be discovered by opening our doors and hearts to people from other Christian faith traditions. Second, I committed to work as hard as possible in turning the church toward an outward-facing mission, rather than to remain internally preoccupied. We would be open and we would be relevant in our community and beyond. Everyone welcome! No navel-gazing, only meaningful action and determined thinking and learning.

My strategy created a good measure of chaos, to say the least. We challenged the notion that we were the only Christians in town. We maintained our love of attempting to be only Christians, just not that we possessed a corner on the market of genuine Christianity. These ideas unsettled the church at its roots. We lost some members. But we also began to grow and change. The new-found freedom and openness we discovered empowered us to serve and reach out to the community. We were open to tackling almost any problem or need. The chaos we created made it all possible. There were no bad ideas. Any dream or vision could be brought forward. Our leadership changed and the church filled with new life. Disruption worked as our members began to expect it.

Much of the time, we work hard to avoid disruptions. And it is important to note that disruption for the sake of disruption seldom accomplishes much. Purposeful disruption linked to mission and progress can affect meaningful change. Responsiveness to your context—social, personal, spiritual, intellectual, missional—demands pliability and tolerance for disruption, intended or not. Disruption results in breakthroughs, essential findings, victories, and, yes, defeats as well along the way. Effective leaders take seriously the ideas, complaints, and opinions of their customers, neighbors, and constituents. Disruption often follows when leaders listen to followers and others. Effective leaders listen. Trust follows listening, and then, disruptive action becomes feasible.

Leaders who are trusted and build their work on honest responsiveness to the challenges that come their way change the world. Don't be afraid of challenging those who look to you for leadership and answers. Just be sure to live your answers and to model consistently the change and the disruption you seek to orchestrate for the good of your mission.

During my years at my home church, we tackled some big issues, especially for a typical congregation. We didn't pull back, no matter how large or controversial the challenge. We asked again and again if our various options and invitations fit our mission and our calling. If they did, we usually went to work, no matter how disruptive. We challenged racism by protesting when then presidential candidate David Duke showed up at our city's civic center for a large, hate-filled rally. We helped Central American refugees who fled the bloody, unjust wars raging in their homelands, wars many considered shameful due to the U.S. involvement on the wrong side of the conflicts. As noted previously, we served and welcomed people living with AIDS. We offered high-quality child care to about 150 families every day of the workweek at some cost to the church. We challenged sectarian theology, and we welcomed all kinds of people from various backgrounds as members. We became known in the community simply as "the CARE Church" (Christians at Richardson East). Notably, one of our oldest and longtime members won the contest for rebranding our congregation with that acronym! The fact that the perception of radical caring followed some measure of internal disruption seemed like a good trade to most of us. The disruption followed and shaped our mission as a group. I use my experience at the church as sort of a parable pointing to the value and the power of being willing to disrupt things for the sake of progress.

One of the most disruptive steps we took involved selling our aging and inadequate church property. For twenty-two months, we met at the First Christian Church (Disciples of Christ) building, a neighboring church. We met on Sunday afternoons, a challenging time and arrangement especially during Cowboys season! After almost two years, we moved into a new facility, and in three years we were debt-free. Our motto during that most disruptive time: *Freedom to Serve*. With little debt and a building designed to more effectively engage our environment, we moved forward grateful for almost every aspect of our challenging disruption.

This same commitment to nurturing and cultivating disruption worked its way into my experience at CitySquare. Ask anyone on our team who's been with us any time at all, and they will tell you disruption remains a vital characteristic of our culture. It's not difficult to make a list of the evidence.

We turned the operation of our food pantry over to the customers of the community who used it on a regular basis. Allowing poor people who need the food and the service to play an integral role in the operation of one of our signature programs creates continual disruption immediately and by definition. In a poverty stricken area, when you basically dismiss outside, suburban, well-to-do volunteers in favor of your poor "service targets," you are in deep disruption!

Mergers with or takeovers of other organizations produce deep disruption. In 2000, at the request of another organization, we took over its operations and worked for a year to merge the new group with our existing team. We considered the move strategic because it ushered us into an area of our city where the need was enormous and where we had long wanted to engage the neighbors who lived there. Blending staff, unifying everyone in a common culture, clearly communicating to the community we entered as newcomers, refining programming plans, releasing some team members and adding others, all added to the dynamic disruption.

But this was a disruption that increased our effectiveness and our footprint in the city. We learned so much and we grew dramatically for taking this discomforting risk.

Sharing aggressively with partners surprises people. Sharing freely disrupts. Years ago, we operated an office in the middle of a public housing development. From that office space, we orchestrated numerous initiatives, mainly for the sake of children and their families. The tough neighborhood offered many daunting challenges. On one occasion, we learned that a "competing" organization needed office space in the same area as our offices. When we learned of their need, we consolidated tightly in half of the space that the housing authority provided us. Then, we invited the other organization to join us. Lots of creative disruption resulted in much better outcomes for the community. It's worth noting that we received this office opportunity because of the merger described above! Disruption pays off.

In about 1998, I distilled what our neighbors told us about the real and pressing need they faced when it came to finding decent and affordable housing into a brief white paper entitled "Hope Street." Almost two years later, John Greenan, one of our lawyers at CitySquare, turned that white paper vision into the Central Dallas Community Development Corporation (now known as CitySquare Housing), a new business endeavor set up to deliver on our neighbors' housing needs. Want to stir up some wonderfully empowering disruption? Start a business in the middle of your nonprofit corporation! The stories we could tell!

But disruption can be observed, remembered, and honored again and again in our organization. Consider this list of disruptive actions we've endured:

- firing long-time team members
- hiring new team members

- living with troubling personalities who didn't believe in our mission
- shuffling effective people to new areas of responsibility
- beginning new efforts
- terminating ineffective or obsolete programs
- opening new offices
- expanding to other cities and learning a new geography and culture
- constructing new buildings
- selling property
- moving

The list goes on and on. Every action noted brings new waves of disruption. Without healthy doses of disruption, your culture and organizational atmosphere will grow stale and lifeless.

To disrupt is to create!

Go for it.

Your Turn

1. How do you feel when someone argues for being intentionally disruptive? Does disruption make you afraid? Confident? Explain.
2. Describe a time when you were involved in a disruptive situation. What was the result? What was negative? What was positive? What was the role of leadership in this experience?
3. Outline two to three situations or challenges in which you feel disruption could be useful. Why do you feel this way?
4. What factors make disruption work?
5. Can you think of leaders whom you respect who often functioned as "disrupters"? Describe some of their work.
6. What would you like to disrupt today? Why?

CHAPTER EIGHTEEN

VALUE THE COUNTERINTUITIVE

Many people who know me would likely agree that I am in a "helping profession." In a certain way, that is exactly true. My job allows me to be in a position to assist people in addressing their problems and meeting their needs. However, I've learned that the most important question to ask a person who comes seeking assistance is typically not asked. My impulse is to ask questions that start with "What? Why? How? Who? Where? When?"

However, the question that I've learned to be most important and that I ask much more frequently is "what if?"

What if you solved your pressing problem today? Can you image that with us? Then what?

We can spend lots of time asking the first six, usually primary questions. But we avoid the counterintuitive query "what if?" because we don't think in terms of a future or a solution or freedom from the snaring difficulty that's been identified before us. Pouring a sense of possibility into the lives of the wonderful people who seek our assistance may be our most important work. Challenging "the needy" to go deep inside to consider the capacity and the wealth within that just might be lying fallow can often change the conversation completely.

Giving people things can be helpful and relatively easy. Pointing out what a person already possesses can be powerful and wildly liberating. Even more importantly, it is imperative that "people helpers" learn to move in a counterintuitive direction with our expectations of those who seek our assistance. Often, we think too small with people. Shame on us when we lapse into such behaviors.

My friend Wendy knows "stuck" up close and personal. She lost her disability benefits due to some technical error she made or some petty crime she committed. Now, she begs for food and lives with a man who abuses her.

What does she need? Sympathy?

I don't think so. What she needs is tough love and concern that won't give up on the one hand nor let her off the hook on the other. Her requests for money to buy what she needs to get by on a daily basis fall on my deaf ears these days. I'm pushing hard for her to go back to the Social Security Administration and fight to get her disability benefits restored, for which she clearly qualifies.

Reversing normalcy, moving in an attractive, but seemingly risky, opposite direction often works wonders. Going off script can be revolutionary. If you want to be useful in human and community renewal, ask those same six questions. But don't fail to ask that last, most important question: What if?

Always seriously consider moving in the opposite direction of what seems obvious, indicated, or traditionally expected. So how does that actually work? Often, you'll recognize the opportunity to move against the grain naturally and almost automatically. At other times, you'll need to work on discovering or creating the pathway you know will make a difference in a person's or a community's life. What is the formula? Consider three steps to discover a start.

Step One: Measure Your Available Assets

To reverse the flow of power and ability in surprising ways, you must understand all the available assets. Don't be fooled into thinking that the only asset or influence in your context is what you bring to the game by yourself. Learn to "asset map" everything: people who arrive with problems; community institutions; resources of all kinds that you seemingly control; friendships with others that could be leveraged to your aid; professional colleagues; team members; and outside-the-box options for everyone involved in the presenting dilemma or pressing need. As you work in this way, you'll discover power allowing you to move into and through often unnoticed seams and passages leading toward surprising results. While this is hard to adequately describe, take it from me: you'll know what I'm talking about when you encounter it.

Step Two: Respect the People Who Seek Your Help by Challenging Them

"Do you want to get better?" is a fair question.

"What are you willing to invest to see the progress in overcoming your problem?" "What can you do, even though in a position of need, to help someone else?" For many people, such questions will be surprising. But by placing the focus on the will of the seeker, a subtle reversal of possibilities begins. Discovery here propels people to new, unimagined outcomes.

Step Three: Expect Big Results

Communicate your expectations. Set in place a way to measure the progress of both the helper and the person seeking assistance. Hold people accountable. Invite those who seek your help to hold you accountable as well. Remember, real friends, neighbors, and colleagues expect to talk straight with each other. Only honesty gets you what everyone desires and needs.

What is true of people from the outside seeking assistance is also true of people on your team of helpers. We move in a counterintuitive direction when we tell our social workers to "blur the lines" and resist the boundaries that professional training routinely proscribes. Establishing friendships with customers can seem risky, but seems to enhance the dynamic necessary to achieve the results we all seek. Our most effective neighbor support services team members turn their process into a fine art.

No matter how long I work among low-income people, I am continually surprised by their courage, resilience, and progress. Often, I don't think in "what if?" terms as consistently as I should.

As noted earlier, a couple of years ago, members of our employment training team approached our leadership team and pitched the idea of providing all our employment training students with financial literacy education. My immediate reaction was negative. "Why waste the students' time doing financial literacy instruction with people who have no money?" I asked with impatience. But the team persisted, wore me down, and got their way, thank goodness! The financial coaching is now baked into all our employment training curricula. The financial results for our students have been amazing and extremely counterintuitive to my expectations. Think about it and it makes perfect sense. Our graduates get jobs. With these jobs come higher wages and regular paychecks, for many students the first paycheck in a long, long time. What is a student to do with the new income? As we work with students to understand goals they set for themselves, we can be helpful in encouraging success as the students define success. Now that they are trained, that is not so much a concern. The results have been so surprising, like most counterintuitive outcomes. All are banked. All are saving. All are making real progress. How terrible if my traditional thinking had carried the day. And this is just one example of counterintuitive action, programming, and movement.

Recently, our willingness to think "strangely" about low-income neighbors and their ability to manage their limited resources led us down a completely new pathway. Our conversation began as we considered applying for a rather sizeable state grant designed to lift people out of poverty. The grant offered over three million dollars annually for a countywide program to lift a specified number of people above the poverty level over a specified period of time. We wrestled with whether to go for the grant. Program expansion requirements, numbers of persons expected to be successful at the end of the grant period, strains on our existing staff, and a host of other issues occupied our rather lively conversation/debate about which direction to take on the grant.

In the midst of the tiring discussion, a crazy idea hit me between the eyes. "What if we raised a 'wealth creation' fund of $1,000,000? Then, what if we identified fifty families or individuals and deposited $20,000 in each of their bank accounts? We could create a 'check back with us' calendar for scheduling reporting sessions on their progress. I bet you that their success rates would outperform our traditional approaches to lifting people out of poverty. What do you all think?" Naturally, everyone stared at me in rational disbelief as usual.

Since that meeting, I've shared the idea with many individuals and several groups. The notion that poor people aren't stupid has been validated so many times in my personal experience that I have no doubt my idea would work. The basis of this backward approach can be observed clearly in third world settings where the poor are given money directly with great results. (To dig deeper programmatically here, search "give money to the poor" on the Internet.)

Months after that staff meeting on the unworkable grant, I received an email message from a wealthy Dallas philanthropist. She wrote, "Larry, I was talking about you recently with someone, can't recall who, and they mentioned that you are interested in giving money to poor people. Well so am I! In fact, I've been thinking about it for a long time and didn't even know there was a movement studying this concept, called Basic Income. Have you been following that? Please stay in touch with me if you want to brainstorm this topic further." I set an appointment, and we are working on the idea with a new level of serious determination.

Just a Brief Word about Counterintuitive Leadership

Jesus shared a number of surprising directions about how to make life work best. Many, if not most or all, of his instructions feel extremely counterintuitive to me. One of my favorite examples speaks to the humility necessary for effective leaders. The scene is set in the home of a wealthy religious leader where Jesus enjoys a meal with his guest. In the middle of the meal, as he watches people no doubt jockeying for positions of honor near the host, Jesus passes along this advice about presumptions:

> When you are invited by someone to a wedding banquet,
> do not sit down at the place of honor, in case someone
> more distinguished than you has been invited by your
> host; and the host who invited both of you may come
> and say to you, "Give this person your place," and then
> in disgrace you would start to take the lowest place. But
> when you are invited, go and sit down at the lowest
> place, so that when your host comes, he may say to you,
> "Friend, move up higher"; then you will be honored in
> the presence of all who sit at the table with you. For all

who exalt themselves will be humbled, and those who humble themselves will be exalted. (Luke 14:8–11 NRSV)

As strange as it sounds, I have experienced this principle at work again and again. This "positioning advice" pays rich dividends to leaders who learn the fine, but counterintuitive practice of taking the lowest seat available.

Your Turn

1. What would acting in a counterintuitive direction mean in your life? Describe.
2. Describe a time when you or someone you know took such action.
3. How do you feel about the risk? On a scale of one to ten, with one being "totally risk-averse" and ten being "always ready to risk it," where do you fall?
4. How important is the "what if?" question? Why?
5. How do people respond to you when you move in a surprising, unthought-of direction?
6. How does failure affect you? Please explain.

CHAPTER NINETEEN

REMEMBER THE MISSION

What is your purpose? What is it you're trying to do? Why does your group, company, or organization exist? Is the activity or work you envision needed now? On what do you base the claim of necessity?

Until you can answer these questions, and a few others like them, don't take another step. Few aspects of life, work, and accomplishment in your organization can rival agreement on a clear understanding of your mission. Once you understand your purpose, it is essential that you craft a concise statement of your mission. The discipline of articulating your mission will assist you in many other aspects of your growth and development as a team and as individual leaders. Mission statements tend to be tricky, presenting unique challenges once a group gets down to doing the tough work of writing, modifying, debating, and arriving at an agreed-upon statement.

So, what are the characteristics of a useful mission statement? Consider these suggested qualities as you create your own, personal mission statement.

Concise

The most effective statement of your mission will be short and simple. The shorter the better, in my view. Your mission statement should form the core of any elevator speech you share with team members who relate to potential and interested donors. Everyone can become a fund developer if they know and can state the mission clearly without wrapping everything in boring, needless detail. Your mission statement should prompt questions that lead your conversation deeper into your work and its challenges. To keep first things first, your mission statement must be simple and memorable. Conciseness makes that possible. I've actually seen "mission walls." By that, I mean literally an entire ten-foot wall used as a giant canvas for a much-too-detailed and lengthy statement of an organization's mission. A mission statement that occupies an entire wall needs to be shortened!

Accurate

This may seem obvious, but a surprising number of organizations don't pursue the mission they claim as descriptive of their actual work. Effective mission statements will invite organizational scrutiny and continuing adjustment to ensure mission fidelity expressed through work that drives the mission as stated and agreed upon. One of the real threats to mission fidelity is "mission creep," a phenomenon that arises when mission and work no longer align. Possibly one of the strongest forces pushing against the fidelity of your mission involves funding decisions. Many sources of support for your work may impose new requirements and bring new sorts of activities along with the much-needed funding. It takes real courage and honest reflection to turn down funding for the sake of faithfulness to the agreed-upon mission focus.

Needed

As noted above, to be effective and worthy of support, the work you undertake should be responding to demonstrable, recognized, clearly documented need. Your mission statement must be strong enough to make the necessity of your work self-evident. Beyond the statement of your mission and purpose, you will want to develop ongoing data to substantiate the need for what you are up to. Equally important, you must continue to seriously evaluate feedback from customers to determine whether your mission remains relevant and necessary. Leaders and organizations must exercise authentic humility to arrive at legitimate answers to such important questions.

Measureable

Everyone on your team must recognize the need to report on what you accomplish. Reporting outputs is important and comparatively easy. The real challenge, though, required more and more frequently by funders these days, involves reporting on outcomes (see Chapter Seven). Not just how many units of work are you accomplishing, but what you can report as the actual impact of your work on a community or a population. For example, it is one thing to report on how many students enrolled for a construction training class. It is another to keep track of the class graduates so that you can report on how many landed jobs, what pay they received, how many remained employed after six months or a year. Or consider financial literacy training. We can easily report how many people completed the class. But the more important question remains: How much did each student manage to save and how many of their personal goals did they achieve by the end of the training and a year later?

A mission statement may seldom contain direct language about measuring results, but the major target of your work needs to allow for this assumption by those investors who give you serious consideration for funding and support. If we exist to fight poverty, how do we intend to measure our victories? And does our mission statement set us up nicely for that part of our enterprise? We've found that measuring outcomes serves to refocus us to stay trained on the bull's-eye of mission accomplishment. Every objective, strategy, and tactic must fold up under and support our mission.

Teachable

Your mission statement must form the basis of not only your fundraising efforts, but it must also be substantial enough to support the weight of all your team training requirements. Every team member should be able to state the organizational mission clearly and effectively. And every team member must be able to converse about your mission and how it drives and shapes the particular work of every member of your team in every department and program. Understanding your mission sets culture.

Understandable

A mission statement must be easy to understand, even with little explanation. At CitySquare, "we fight the causes and effects of poverty through direct service, advocacy, and friendship." We've found this short statement adequate for addressing the purpose questions that staff, neighbors, and donors seek to answer. It leads us to clearly articulate any or all our program agendas and activities while providing a pathway into public policy and systemic change that promise poverty reduction. We consider friendship the "secret sauce" our organization applies to ensure human connection. It remains an essential part of the meal we serve to our community. This simple statement begs important questions we eagerly seek to answer and to discuss, sometimes ad infinitum, ad nauseum! Our previous mission statement was much more ambiguous and went something like (not so memorable, actually) "we exist to share the love of God in word, action, and attitude while building genuine community in the neighborhoods where we live and work." Compared to our current, rather clean and certain statement, the old line just didn't allow us to hit the target often enough. And it led us down many rabbit trails unconnected to our actual programming efforts.

If I could construct a model of our organization with the mission positioned at the center of the construction, I'd need a circular platform, four pillars, a broad base, and a marquee. I know this sounds strange, and possibly only grandparents can understand. Bear with me here. On the circular platform, I would mount the marquee that listed in bright lights the three key elements of our mission: "Direct service, advocacy, and friendship discovered here!" Beneath the circular platform with marquee installed and lighted, I would attach four strong pillars with top to bottom banners hanging attractively, each labeled clearly with one of our four areas of concern: hunger, health, housing, and hope. The pillars would then be attached to the strong, broad base that would be inscribed with a brief description of the populations with whom we work: low-income, working poor; homeless, disabled adults; and low-income youth who age out of the state foster care system. Population groups, measureable deliverables, and a clear and certain mission—that is my model.

My final piece of advice relates to the importance of objectivity and your organizational commitment to reflection and brutal honesty. Not everything works. When something fails, admit it. Call failure what it is. A commitment to honest self-reflection and an openness to outside evaluation will be important tools in staying on mission. We've experienced many failures and countless false starts. I've noticed over the years that when we are most attuned to our real, agreed upon mission, we fail less often, and when we do fail, we recover more quickly and rebound with renewed purpose and commitment, often thanks to what we've learned by our stumble. We've chased some crazy ideas across the years. We pursued irrelevant funding that boxed us in and limited us. We've redirected program goals in ways that weren't in keeping with our values. We actually attempted to turn our legal center into a social enterprise to help address a funding shortage created by our rapid growth. As I write and reflect on it honestly, the most threatening distraction an organization faces is the temptation to chase funding, even if the pursuit leads to a departure from your true north, your mission. Don't let that happen. Build honest evaluation processes into your teams and your culture so that you can stay on course.

You'll never regret being sold out to your mission.

You will always regret surrendering your true purpose to something less than your heart's best hope and clearest vision.

Your Turn

1. What is the mission statement of an organization with which you are closely associated? Could it be improved? How? Why do you say that?
2. Do you have a personal mission statement that guides your life? Explain and reflect on it if you do.
3. Think about a time when mission clarity served you well, even to the point of providing helpful protection. Describe the incident or experience.

4. Describe a time when you departed from your mission. What happened? What were the short-term and long-term results/consequences?
5. How important is knowing and fully embracing your mission statement or that of your group? Why?
6. In your experience, how important is it for an organization that all team members understand and engage in the realization of its mission? Explain.

SERVE CUSTOMERS

Working in the nonprofit sector presents unique challenges. One of the most formidable has to do with community relations and the basic issue of how we treat and regard the people who come to us with lots of problems. These are the men, women, and children who seek our assistance in solving their problems, or at least making them more bearable.

Who are these people to us?

Cases to be managed?
Data points to be entered and tracked?
Potential outcomes to be reported?
Sick people to be healed?
Workers to be trained?
Tenants to be housed?
Clients to be represented?
Hungry neighbors to be fed?
Children to be guided and involved?

While each of these descriptions presents a measure of truth about the people who show up at our door, none feel adequate when laid down on our strategy table alongside our values and our mission.

Neighbors as Customers

No, at the end of the day, every person who seeks us out must be regarded by every person on our team first and foremost as a customer. I've known for many years that, especially in a poverty-fighting organization like CitySquare, it is imperative that we treat people like customers.

Now, customers can be demanding. Customers have been known to complain, right? Customers want choice and variety. Customers expect to be treated with respect and helpfulness. Customers look for politeness when they come by to shop. It's all true.

For years, I've counseled our team that if the people who come our way aren't complaining about something, then we aren't doing enough to convey to them that we regard them as our customers, our reason to exist. This is true for a number of reasons. For one thing, almost all our neighbors who seek our help pay something for our services. We learned years ago that if people have a genuine, usually monetary, investment in the process, they will keep their commitments, as well as their appointments. At the same time, they expect us to keep ours. That means they are our customers and, as such, they have the right to expect our best in customer service and genuine respect.

We've discovered power in the surprise that often washes over people when they recognize that we consider them to be our customers and that we intend to meet their needs in the best way possible. Furthermore, we are committed to checking in with them to make sure we are performing adequately.

Little things begin to have great impact when we work under this assumption. I remember the first time I said "thanks for coming by" to a poor, homeless man who waited on his turn to shop in our food center. The shock on his face quickly gave way to delight as he realized the high regard we had for him, his concerns, his opinions, and his problems. Such an expression changed the entire dynamic of our encounter. The power shifted to him and away from us. He got the message that we were glad he came, and we would be pleased if he came again!

Improvements in our food center, as just one example, allow it to feel and to present more like a real grocery store than a food pantry. I've enjoyed amazing conversations with customers about the changes we've made. Asking a mother who comes to shop "How do you like the changes we've made?" conveys clearly that we've made the improvements with her in mind, renovates the entire atmosphere, and breathes new life into the entire place and into every exchange with shoppers. Or by asking "Are we treating you right?" or "Do you have suggestions about how to make it better yet?" we convey the simple truth behind our clear mission—we fight poverty by relating to our friends and neighbors as customers. Customer satisfaction surveys are always helpful. The simple fact that we ask people how they feel about their experiences with us demonstrates clearly that we believe the customer is always right.

Donors as Customers

We have another group of customers, and we depend on them for all that we do. Since we don't make widgets to sell, we count on various funding sources to underwrite our work. Donors come in all forms, shapes, and sizes. Public dollars involve grants and contracts, reports, audits, site visits, and skills training to prepare our team to satisfy the conditions of the essential funds. Private funds come from individuals, churches and faith communities, foundations, corporations, United Way, some fee-for-service dollars, as mentioned, and receipts from a couple of our own social enterprises.

In each case, we identify another set of customers with whom to contend and to serve. Thanking these customers for coming by is easy enough. But to truly serve them, we go to great lengths to expose them to the fullness and complexities of our work and our world. We work hard to create space in which interested donors can explore and learn without inappropriately invading the space and work of our community customers. We spend time attempting to educate our donor customers about the hard realities facing our impoverished neighbors who are community customers. Often, the simple framing of this customer-provider dynamic opens up new understandings to our underwriters and investors. Every report we submit, every item of data we explain, and every surprise we describe or reveal are essential portions of our customer service to the donors.

Increasingly, we find ourselves at the magic intersection of donor customer and community customer in direct contact with one another. When we find ourselves in this special space, we've come to expect breakthroughs, if not an occasional miracle that always seems to benefit all our customers—consumers and investors—and certainly our team.

The fact is, we have a product. We call it human and community development. We work hard at selling it. Over the years, we've discovered that respect is everything. We've witnessed this truth with the materially poor. Nothing changes things, heals wounds, or instills hope quite like respect. When respect is present, no one need point it out. Respect tends to be a self-evident game changer. Interestingly, respect works the same way with the wealthy who share their own, often unrecognized, wounds and needs with the community of our neighbors. When our donor customers and our community customers discover and act out mutual respect, we find ourselves on the right path to lasting change and to deep community renewal. We believe that one way to promote community health and well-being all around is to serve all our customers so well that they will tell their friends who will join them in the special spaces CitySquare provides.

Your Turn

1. How does it feel to be treated as a valued customer? What are the essential elements in creating that experience for you?
2. How do you feel about regarding those you and your organization serve as customers? What are the challenges? What attitudes do you expect to encounter? Or do you and your team already seek to do that?
3. What changes would be necessary for your organization to begin treating those you serve like customers?
4. How do you feel about regarding donors/funders as customers? What changes would be necessary for your organization to begin treating those who give to your mission like customers?
5. How disruptive would the changes suggested here be for you, your team, and the organization with which you work? Explain.

CHAPTER TWENTY-ONE

NO STUPID QUESTIONS

Most of us don't enjoy the feelings that go along with the sense that we have a stupid question that needs to be asked and answered one way or the other. Understandably, we don't want to risk being considered ill-informed, illogical, or just plain stupid. So, far too often, we remain quiet when discussions with others invite these questions. Isn't it strange how we feel sympathetic and even encouraging to others who risk it and go ahead and ask a question that might be considered less than insightful? This is clearly a reluctance we just need to get over!

There really are no stupid questions.

From so-called stupid questions, we gain new insights that propel new action in the service of our mission. Questioning almost always leads to progress, new understandings, and deeper connections to our teammates. At the very least, such questions often prompt enlivening laughter and joy!

So how do leaders promote an organizational culture that values questions, no matter how elementary they may sound or seem?

Leaders Foster a Culture of Open-Hearted Inquiry

Applauding the team member who brings questions to the task before him can set the organizational expectation that questions will be welcomed, expected, and rewarded. By taking questions seriously, leaders communicate just how important it is for everyone to adopt inquisitive approaches to problems and suggested solutions. Expressing thanks, both publicly and privately, to employees who are willing to ask questions communicates to the team your leadership's value of questions, no matter their nature. Often, simple questions advance us more than the obtuse or complicated questions. Curiosity ought to be celebrated, singled out, and rewarded whenever we observe it at work.

Leaders Never Hear Stupid Questions

People need to understand. Often, we are each at a different position up and down the understanding scale of any issue on the table or up for discussion. People with long histories in the organization or field of expertise add invaluable insights about how things are done, what things mean or signal, and what the organizational culture is all about. In a similar way, newcomers arrive with fresh, outside perspectives to make available to their new organization. The wise leader never makes fun of anyone. Doubly damaging are leaders who make honest questioners feel stupid, unappreciated, and without merit. Leaders who routinely respond to questions in a condescending or superior manner may be revealing their own insecurity and not the limitations of the person who brings an honest inquiry to the group. Strong, effective, and respected leaders invite all questions.

Leaders Regard No Question as Off-Limits or Out-of-Bounds

Of course, I'm not referring to ill-mannered, insulting, rude, or obviously irrelevant questions when I say no questions are off-limits. But, as to the mission, strategy, and tactics of the team, the more questions the better. The more far-reaching the inquiry, the better for leaders who seek to exploit the knowledge and the curiosity of the entire team. Questioning organizations innovate, attempt new things, and evaluate honestly, all with the goal of improving performance and driving positive outcomes for the entire team toward the mission. Teams that are unafraid to ask the wildest, most unusual questions are teams that accomplish new and surprising things.

Leaders Invite Everyone to Solve Problems

At CitySquare, our president and chief operating officer, Dr. John Siburt, routinely calls program leaders to "COD"—collaborate or die—sessions. He knows that by working across traditional lines of authority and function, we will arrive at great solutions to the challenges we face. The essence of these COD sessions involves us asking questions and grappling with answers. John urges us to question everything. As a result, we often find fresh answers and more effective approaches to the work we undertake. Not surprisingly, these COD sessions create an atmosphere of acceptance. Our team bonds around questioning and problem-solving.

Leaders Question the Way Things Are Done

Effective organizations continually engage in self-reflection, introspection, and evaluation. Teams who routinely question themselves and their work process end up being committed to improvement and progress. When nothing about our work process is sacred in and of itself, the door remains open for new ways of doing things for the sake of our customers, our investors, and our fellow teammates. Questioning precedes progress. Possibly the questions we want to ask about why we do things in a certain way are the questions that most often make us feel stupid. Rule of thumb for leaders: encourage the question. Rule of thumb for team members: ask the question. Questions allow us to respectfully challenge the status quo, especially in regard to those decisions and processes that define our work, what we attempt, and how we attempt it. One of the best things a leader can model for her team occurs as she asks challenging questions about ideas, programs, and strategies that everyone knows began first as her ideas!

Leaders Move throughout the Organization to Encourage Questioning

Spotlighting questions and questioners, no matter from where they come to us, encourages everyone to inquire about anything and any policy. Working with team members closest to the community or with those who've recently joined your team offers a great opportunity for leaders to deepen their understandings of their team members and of the rich talent to be mined from the organization in regard to new and better ways of doing business.

Questions possess a particular power. In and of themselves, questions imply that a commitment to discovery will never die in your organization and among its members and leaders.

There are no stupid questions. To the contrary, all honest questions either lead to brilliant, new understandings and innovations or confirm the value of the way things are understood currently.

Never stop with the questions, already!

Your Turn

1. Recall a time when you felt as if you asked a stupid question. How did you feel? How did those feelings affect your willingness to ask additional questions?
2. Have you witnessed someone ask a question that was then rejected by a leader as stupid or unimportant? Explain.

3. How does the notion that there are no stupid questions strike you?
4. Do you see the connection between an openness to any question and the achievement of innovation and performance and process improvement? Explain.
5. What sort of leader encourages questioning? Explain your impressions.
6. In your experience, what happens when organizations shut down questioning? Share your story.

CHAPTER TWENTY-TWO

VERTICAL TRUMPS HORIZONTAL

Every effective, active, aggressive leader knows anxiety and even fear on personal, intimate terms. Risk accompanies big efforts, almost by definition. The leader who never worries, who falls into bed and sleeps soundly until dawn every night, may need to evaluate the quality and usefulness of his agenda. In such a case, mission adjustment might be worth serious consideration.

We don't talk enough about fear.

That's always seemed strange to me since all of us experience it. And, if we allow it rule over our lives, fear will block us, robbing us of the strength we need to endure and to thrive.

I know well the demoralizing instinct that paralyzes a person between the sheets early in the morning. Somehow, and only for a brief period, a false security surrounds me as long as I lie still and horizontal with my head covered while clutching my pillow. I've discovered that there is no lasting comfort, no driving out fear, no attitude adjustment or creative liberty to be found so long as I'm off my feet. Horizontal may feel satisfying for a moment, but lingering parallel to the ground only turns up the flow of stomach acids and self-doubt.

On the other hand, when I resolve to get up, to stand on my feet, to face the day (almost always with the help of a hot cup of coffee), I find that my fears and my anxiety fall into much healthier alignment, including a much more workable perspective.

My literal assessment of the value of standing up may sound strange to you. But I can assure you, I find new hope and wondrous possibilities every time I rise to face my fear, whatever it may be. You may develop or already employ a completely different mental image to understand and to use as you take concrete action against your fear. That's great. Just make sure that whatever your tool(s) is for facing down your fear that you engage in that battle directly and aggressively.

In short, for me, vertical trumps horizontal.

And goodness knows, I've had plenty of reason to fear over the course of my career. Listing exhaustively the sources of my anxiety makes me fearful! I mean, I've done some embarrassing, crazy, and at times foolish stuff across the years. Each example would take me several pages to flesh out. So, I'll just keep it simpler than it likely is; but still you'll get the point, I expect.

Here's my list—we might call it my "whatever you do, no matter how bothersome, stay vertical today when you do this stuff" list:

- ✓ Things I've said in public for lots of people to hear
- ✓ Essays and articles I've written on controversial subjects
- ✓ Projects I've tackled, many of them controversial and against the grain of the status quo

- ✓ People I've associated with, stood up for, and included
- ✓ Mistakes I've made
- ✓ Feelings I've hurt
- ✓ People I've overlooked
- ✓ Decisions I've made
- ✓ Assumptions I've erroneously acted upon
- ✓ Friends I've lost
- ✓ Details I've overlooked
- ✓ Folks I've angered or offended
- ✓ Resources I've wasted
- ✓ Traditions I've discounted or made fun of
- ✓ Times I've been rude
- ✓ Social media I've fired out with too little wisdom, care, or thought

My list could go on and on. And to make things worse, my lists morph, and at times I don't even recognize my reality accurately enough to anticipate things of which I should be afraid. But I know fear.

To be a bit more concrete, I'll mention a few examples of situations that have made me afraid to get out of bed in the morning.

511 N. Akard

The fifteen-story, abandoned office tower that we bought, financed, and redeveloped in mixed-use fashion that included two hundred units of extremely affordable housing (including over one hundred formerly homeless individuals) caused me, from start to finish, to lose lots of sleep! In addition, we developed six units of upscale, market-rate condo living space on the top floor. Then, we added three floors and a basement of office/retail space. Mixed-income, mixed-use rental property located in the middle of downtown

Dallas—what could possibly go wrong? And that's just the development process; it says nothing about managing the property day to day!

During the development planning process, the financing of the deal caused almost unspeakable anxiety for John Greenan, the director of our housing division, and for me. One thing always seemed tethered to something else; and in every case, the failure of one aspect of the deal threatened the success and survival of the entire enterprise. The entire effort became a high-stakes juggling act. I spent a good deal of middle-of-the-night horizontal time, trying to imagine in the dark how the project could ever work out. But it did.

No matter how dire the situation might seem, or how strange it may sound to you, standing up always made things better for me. Hear me here: the physical act of standing up cleared my head, but even more, my mind and my spirit. Maybe it's just me, but nothing ever seemed as bad or as overwhelming from a vertical position.

News Media

I love news media people. I find them extremely interesting, and mostly helpful, most of the time. At the same time, news stories offer real challenges. My bias has always been to open up everything to media whose job it is to tell the important stories of a community.

Yet, working closely with media can be nerve-racking, if for no other reason than they have such a limited and ever-shrinking amount of space and time to tell their stories. My commitment to open up the entire story is seldom matched by a news person's available space in column inches or in elapsed time on a screen. Add to this space limitation the fact that some of our stories have been critical of community priorities, and therefore controversial, and you have another recipe for anxiety and stress. Wanting the story to run tomorrow morning is understandable. Waiting until morning to read the final copy can be an ordeal. Online media postings made in advance of the printed newspaper or electronic versions posted online prior to an actual broadcast, or both preserved there permanently, combine to arouse worry and seconding-guessing your input or performance.

In almost every case across the years, my worry and fear have been exaggerated through the night. Every time I face such a circumstance, I do better if I will simply stand up and go to work.

Developing good relationships with media personalities is essential. Telling them everything you know and exactly what you know is almost always the right thing to do, unless you are holding a confidence for someone else. It is amazing how much better I do at remembering my commitments to media friends and realizing that they are professional colleagues and truth tellers when I am out of the fetal position encouraged by my bed.

Social Media

The relatively recent advent of 24/7 social media platforms allows for instantaneous reactions to news events from around the world, as well as gossip of any local community or group. Blogs encourage longer pieces of communication. Facebook and Twitter provide quick and easy pathways for communicating ideas, questions, opinions, and arguments, to say nothing of snide, rude, and sometimes crude remarks and criticisms.

I've posted some stupid ideas on social media platforms, some of which caused me more of the anxiety I'm describing here. I am a news junkie. The ability to engage in a story, often in real time, can become addictive, and a waste of time. The loss of sleep sometimes follows my overwrought expressions of opinion that often could just as well go unexpressed. I've learned that some of the anxiety with which I deal could be avoided if I just kept my mouth shut and my hands away from the computer or iPad!

Vertical Is Just Better

What is it about my physical posture that brings me relief? Why is vertical so much better for me? And let me say again, it may not be your preferred practice. You may achieve a similar or even better outcome by remaining horizontal or on your knees somewhere between vertical and horizontal. Whatever your response to fear, find the practice that equips you and works for you in the process of overcoming debilitating fear. As my weapon of choice against fear, I've at least discovered a few of the reasons why being upright works for me.

Faith and Faithfulness Are about Action and Movement

As a leader, you have to find ways to believe in your source of power, in your mission, in your team, and, yes, in yourself. For me, standing up affirms my actual willingness to continue in my appointed work. When knocked down by fear or criticism or failure or loss of dwindling resources, whatever the problem or the challenge, standing up embodies my recommitment to carry on! The psychosomatic reality of standing on my feet serves me well. When I stand up, I stare down my fear and I'm able to move forward with more clarity, resolve, and determination. If fear can't keep me down, it can never defeat me.

Standing Almost Always Follows a Clear, Simple Prayer for Mercy

Standing up has little if anything to do with my ability or my strength. I find that I am able to stand only because, in my extremity, my first thought every morning is to cry out simply for mercy. The older I grow and the further I walk, the simpler my prayers have become. Before standing up, I utter my litany of requests summed up in a one-word mantra, "Mercy." My prayers sound like this every new day: "Lord, I'm getting up again. I can't stay in the bed. I can't stay on my back. I'm standing up now. Mercy, Lord, sweet mercy, let me stand."

My Best Thinking Is Upright

Sitting at my writing table with journal open before me or "mind dump" sheet at my side for updates and additional action items for my day, I find peace, calm, and rising eagerness to battle the day ahead, including the apologies, clarifications, and revisions made necessary by the day I enjoyed yesterday. Morning air, hot coffee, and assurance of mercy prepare me for the best time of the day—another chance to do my work with a commitment to clearer, higher-quality thoughts.

Being Upright Reminds Me of People Who Count on Me

I cannot stay down. Too many precious people expect me to get up again today and do my thing as they do theirs. Whether at home, at school, at work, in the community/neighborhood, or in church, I get up because other important people need me to—they are counting on me. How dare I stay down because of anxiety, fear, or suffocating self-doubt? So I say to myself just before I rise, "Stand up, man! You dare not waste this day!"

Standing Up to Face My Fear Is the Opposite of Running from Fear

In fact, standing up provides me the assurance I need to know that I'm ready to deal with my reality, no matter how hard, negative, or challenging. Nothing can be gained for long by avoiding my fear. I stand, at least in part, to disable the fears I face. So, don't be afraid. Stand up for the battle!

Your Turn

1. What do you fear most? Why?
2. How do you deal with and address your fears?
3. Ever experience "low-grade" fear? You know, routine anxiety. Describe it.
4. How do fear and self-doubt affect your work as a leader?
5. If not standing up, what metaphor or symbol would you use to overcome or to deal with your fear? Explain.
6. How does prayer or meditation factor into your own ability to master your fear, or do they?

CHAPTER TWENTY-THREE

ACT BEYOND YOUR REACH

On May 25, 1961, President John F. Kennedy gave a speech before a joint session of Congress in which he offered the nation and its leaders a bold, daring challenge. His words still inspire:

> Finally, if we are to win the battle that is now going on around the world between freedom and tyranny, the dramatic achievements in space which occurred in recent weeks should have made it clear to us all, as did the Sputnik in 1957, the impact of this adventure on the minds of men everywhere, who are attempting to make a determination of which road they should take. . . . I believe that this nation should commit itself to achieving the goal, before this decade is out, of landing a man on the moon and returning him safely to the Earth. No single space project in this period will be more impressive to mankind or more important for the long-range exploration of space; and none will be so difficult or expensive to accomplish.[1]

I remember well the excitement prompted by the president's statement. Even more, I recall the pride and the excitement ensuing from the success of the Apollo 11 mission when, on July 20, 1969, three men landed on the moon. As I think about this amazing accomplishment, I remain astonished. Kennedy exemplifies a leader who acted well beyond his personal reach.

Courageous action, against the limits we know far too well and the odds those limits impose, distinguishes effective leaders from those content to fall back into mediocrity, explanations, and inaction. Breakthrough efforts seldom begin with adequate resources for the task. Shortages, inadequacy, and the real fear of running out—these are realities all leaders face. What differentiates great leaders from run-of-the-mill placeholders seems fairly obvious.

Attitude

As we consider the great benefits that accrue to the leader who acts boldly in the face of daunting opportunity, we find ourselves face-to-face with the inestimable necessity of the power of faith. Acting beyond the limits we face is the way of faith. Nothing truly transformative gets done without a bit of old-fashioned, how shall I say, "attitude." Kennedy's bold proposal sent his critics away to contemplate their political gains in the wake of his seemingly preposterous proposal. The speech preceded the accomplishment by a little over eight years, with just under six months to spare, as the deadline of the decade approached. But the president defied logic, the pundits, the cost, and all odds to cast a strong vision through to a successful, world-changing conclusion. Like President Kennedy, even though Oswald snuffed out his life two-and-a-half years after he cast the vision, effective leaders possess attitudes with enough edge to empower and to enable real breakthroughs, sometimes even beyond their own lifetimes. Successful leaders also possess enough brains and expertise within themselves and the teams they call together to have an honest shot at great accomplishment. At the heart of such an attitude, you'll find faith, the sort of trust that stands up against the odds and holds up the team flag of unquenchable hope, and unstoppable determination.

Assumptions

Acting upon and out of the reservoir of an attitude that rejects any notion of what's impossible, leaders assume that anything can be done. Again, faith drives this worldview. Fear is a reaction to what life brings; it is not a worldview. The assumptions growing out of faith provide an understanding of the world and of life that serves to make the impossible not only possible but the new norm or the routine. If I operate out of the assumption that my team can accomplish anything, where then are the limits? Acting beyond my reach with a realistic hope of success means that nothing is too big to be addressed. Further, I can lead and direct my team with the certain expectation that together our prospects of achieving success always fall in the "more than likely" category. If we fail, we fail, but only to fight again. As I noted earlier, if a leader or a team never fail, more than likely the goal is too timid and the vision too small (see Chapter One).

Access and Assessment

Nothing significant happens without access to necessary resources. One of the primary responsibilities of a leader is to assemble the assets needed to accomplish the work envisioned. To be sure, the leader cannot be the sole source for resource development. Effective leaders discern and mine the capabilities of team members when it comes to necessary assets to accomplish the team's mission. It amazes me to observe people with frontline responsibilities who seldom think seriously or consistently about developing access to needed resources. Everyone has access to resources. Everyone should take seriously the wealth available and there for the taking.

What sort of resources and access are necessary for success?

Access to Effective Partnerships Cannot Be Overestimated

As noted previously, effective leaders engage the wealth of as many personal relationships as possible. Further, leaders who get things done also engage systems for the good of their efforts. Social networks, political groupings, public leaders, spiritual and faith communities, educational assets, service sector allies and competitors, family connections, friends, and peers—effective leaders take full advantage of any and all access they enjoy to any and all who will give them a hearing regarding their need for sufficient assets to get the job done.

Resources Follow Quality of Work Already Accomplished

Some of my colleagues and even team members fear any discussion of assessment of performance along the way to mission fulfillment. I understand. It's hard work to measure what you do. But it's also intimidating because at times what you have to report from open, honest assessment is not all that encouraging! Rather than face the possibility of negative results that can come from measurement, some leaders resist, delay, or refuse honest assessment. Bad strategy! And for at least two reasons.

First, virtually every funder requires feedback based on honest, accepted standards of measurement as to the quality of the work being supported by outside assets. Realistic leaders understand correctly that the days of no measurements are long gone.

Second, working hard to report progress, setbacks, and adjustments almost always leads to deepened relationships. When we get good reports, we have a story to tell about the need to fund expansion. When we receive a less-than-expected report, we have an opening to invite supporters in even closer in hopes they can assist in improving our performance.

Honest evaluation leads to new options. Taking a hard look at the propulsion system while we cling to the vision of seeing a man step onto the lunar surface seems more than obvious. New opportunities typically arise from clear evaluation. Time and again, I've watched as the hard work of evaluation pushed us toward new movement, better performance, and out into whatever our "beyond" might be at any given time. Access only grows when we remain committed to assessment.

Action

Develop in your life and in your organization a radical bias for action. A culture of discovery, even when it begins modestly, leads to action far beyond what may have been imagined at the start. Countless small victories and defeats preceded the moon shot. It is certainly true in the organizations I've worked with and led that many significant projects and achievements started out in almost embryonic form. Teams I've been on were responsible for all sorts of efforts and attempts to serve low-income people and families in an almost endless number of ways, through countless circumstances and opportunities. We believe it is best to just do something!

Years ago, at the request of the Dallas Police Department, we created a day labor, "catch out" hall in our food pantry. We opened our doors to the Corporation for National and Community Service's AmeriCorps program. We signed up to recycle paper and boxes, and we sold the idea to partner churches that agreed to locate recycle dumpsters on their property with the proceeds coming back to us. We created a thrift store on a parking lot in the back of one of our centers. Today, the store is a bustling enterprise in an actual retail facility.

Be warned! Decisions over time to take small steps directed by an organizational commitment to discovery will lead to results that are much, much larger and more significant than you may be able to imagine as you begin. Each of the relatively small accomplishments noted above served as precursors to much bigger things. World-changing leaders seldom pause to consider stopping their work. Wise leaders think often about transitions and successors. If rooted in a culture of discovery-informed action, leaders who get things done will find renewal at their fingertips for important work beyond the reach of their beginnings.

Your Turn

1. Consider a time when you took the risk necessary to act beyond your reach. What were the details? How did you feel? What was the outcome?
2. Have you ever been surprised by the unexpected result of your work? What surprised you? Why?
3. How are leaders limited? Make a list!
4. How do you feel leaders overcome their limitations?
5. Name the organizational barriers you've faced in attempting to act beyond what seemed reasonable given your reach.
6. How do you challenge the limits you discover as you do and plan your work? What have you found to be the most important factor(s) in accomplishing surprising results?

NOTE

[1] "May 25, 1961: JFK's Moon Shot Speech to Congress," Space.com, http://www.space.com/11772-president-kennedy-historic-speech-moon-space.html.

CHAPTER TWENTY-FOUR

STICK TO YOUR PROMISE

We've learned the tangible benefit of "brand promise." Organizations like CitySquare reach a point in their development where they must extend a commitment to their community as to who they are and what they intend to do. Several years ago, The Richards Group in Dallas led us through a brand change that included a new name and clearer statements and understandings of our vision, our position in the community, our personality, and who it was we could expect to attract to our mission. Here's how the professional marketing company understood us, after months of conversation and analysis.

BRAND VISION

Changing the trajectory of people's lives

BRAND POSITIONING

To those who want to help the poor, CitySquare
is the local nonprofit organization that
partners with people to improve their lives

BRAND PERSONALITY
Compassionate, gritty, and fiercely committed

BRAND AFFILIATION
People who want in the fight

The Richards Group helped us immeasurably, especially with increased clarity in self-understanding. The process taught me that for leaders, such an endeavor should be ongoing and can be applied with benefit to the various parts of any team serious about mission.

When I talk about the "brand promise" of our housing company, CitySquare Housing, I sketch out a five-step pathway toward understanding what we promise as an organization and how we deliver our work product. In the case of housing development, I begin with "experience" as I point to the numerous projects we've rolled out from design and land acquisition all the way through to completion and operations. Next, I spotlight our "competency" and our "creativity" in working the unique complexities of every project. A simple explanation of how we've gotten creative with the complex capital stacks of our financing goes a long way toward cementing helpful partnerships and new connections to investors, donors, and interested parties. There is no room for pride or bragging here, just a presentation of the facts of each case. Along the way, I touch upon "community relationships" and "trust" by illustrating the various steps we've taken to build, rebuild, and sustain a clear sense of the essential nature of trust and community connection. Our obvious "commitment to growth" is important. We don't intend to stop developing housing, and our commitment to grow assures our customers and our community that we are "all in" as an organization. This is what we do. Finally, we spotlight all our partnerships and our fundamental, systemic commitment to celebrating and growing "great partnerships" to do and to continue our work. Spelling out in detail what drives you and your company will be important to your growth, sustainability, and success.

Lessons Learned

We've learned so much since 1988 at CitySquare. Everything we've experienced has played an important role in our learning. Here are just a few lessons that continue to define us:

- Risk is a prerequisite to progress. Don't fool yourself or waste time debating the point. No risk, no progress.
- Embrace growth and celebrate disruption. Growth means people advance. Disruption almost always signals the advent of new days, new ways, and hope fulfilled.
- The community must respect and trust you. Without the community's sign-off on your presence and your work, you can do little that's transformative, lasting, or significant.
- Tenacity is a given. Tough work demands tough people when it comes to sticking to the work and the vision.
- Get creative. Don't settle for the "tried and true."
- Test your faith. You will be surprised. Your life will grow in surprising ways and in unexpected directions.
- Treasure your partners. Few things are more important in community development.
- Don't be afraid to fail. Don't see yourself as too big to fail—you certainly can and you definitely will. Just don't fear failure. Failure can become your guide, your muse, and your wisdom.
- Remember for whom you work. God. People. Community. Your team.

Sticking to your promise and remaining true to your values and to your heart will serve you well. You'll be known as the person, the people, and the organization that gets things done, that takes care of business.

Hang on, you're in for a wild and wonderful ride!

Your Turn

1. What is your brand promise as an organization? As an individual? Look back over the aspects that comprise this promise.
2. Do you need to create such a promise? What will it contain?
3. What about your brand promise needs to change? Why?
4. What about your brand promise serves you well? Explain your answer.
5. How might a brand promise serve your surrounding community? How about your team?
6. Why could such self-understanding be important to you?
7. Could a clear brand promise help you in attracting partners? How?

CHAPTER TWENTY-FIVE

CLEAN HANDOFF

Starting anything worthwhile brings challenges.

Sustaining what you create and launch moves the intensity and the grind of your challenge into an entirely new dimension. Sustaining your work/organization with the necessary ongoing support gets complicated, often in extremely tedious, often personal ways. After all, payday looms over you again at the end of this pay period!

Developing and implementing a plan for leadership succession in your organization will be one of the most important, if not the most important, tasks you will undertake. One of the most important requirements of an effective leader is her ability to transfer the mantle of leadership and decision-making to the new leader for the next generation.

Founding leaders, and representatives of that generation within an organization, don't always embrace the process or the outcomes of leadership handoff. Founding leaders often find it hard if not impossible to orchestrate this essential transition. This organizational reshuffle proves so difficult for many founding leaders that the process adopted by many groups simply writes the role for founding leader out of the leadership transfer equation. In this strategy, the retiring leader exits before the replacement effort gets underway. A better approach, if possible, engages the departing leader in a period of transition from old to new with lots of celebration.

Why Is Succession So Difficult?

For sure, moving from one leader to the next, particularly when the leader to be replaced has been in the position from the start or for a long time, presents challenges. What are some of the major difficulties?

Set Culture/New Culture

In most cases, the old leader created a culture with predicable dependencies and many unquestioned ways of doing things. In transitions, any change of procedure, policy, or practice can become a point of conflict leading to open disagreements, disputes, and contentious debates. Ironically, organizations set themselves up for conflict precisely because their chosen new leader deserves serious consideration. Every effective leader sets culture, usually in ways that adjust the inherited culture of the organization. Passive-aggressive behavior on the part of the outgoing leader is not unusual and should be addressed clearly and honestly. The old leader who remains in an organization as a new leader arrives must be aware of the consequences of his own good work and learn the fine art of stepping aside in support of the new leader's efforts to adjust or to completely overhaul the organization's culture and strategy going forward. Effective teams own their culture. Clarity about that culture is extremely important. The new leader must be given the space, the freedom, and the time to make the cultural adjustments she feels appropriate and necessary. As the new leader takes over, the departing leader should do everything possible to support and champion the efforts and the vision of incoming leadership. Organizations that promote from within often find it easier to make the leadership transfer due to the fact that the rising leader played a part of setting the culture and the operational values of the team long before assuming the top leadership position.

Surrender Indispensability

The leader who has been at the work of an organization for a long time (ten years or longer) may find it easy, as well as satisfying, to consider himself indispensable. After all, the long-tenured leader usually can rightly take some measure of credit for the organization's growth, accomplishments, and progress. Effective long-term leaders receive feedback that often substantiates such self-appraisals. And this sense of being necessary to the future health and well-being of the organization often lurks beneath the level of consciousness of the outgoing leader. The departing leader may behave with a weird sense of unrecognized entitlement when it comes to this sense of having been and now being essential to the past, present, and future success of the team. Any transition of leadership from a tenured leader to a next-generation leader must take feelings of indispensability seriously. Retiring leaders will benefit from coaching sessions and personal counseling with a professional who understands organizational leadership and the various human dynamics that go along with change. Leaders who prepare for effective transfer of authority take seriously the temptation to consider themselves indispensable. The fact is, while everyone is important and, in many ways, essential, no one is indispensable or irreplaceable. Talking through the emotions of this humbling truth ought to be a normal part of team development in every effective organization. The founding or long-term leader benefits more than anyone by having a healthy and appropriate assessment of his role in the overall work of his team. Ego inflation must be checked for the good of everyone. We've all known of old leaders attempting to sabotage their successors. Such behavior cannot be tolerated. Harsh action, adjustments in your plan, and even termination may be indicated in extreme cases.

Failure to Embrace a New Role

Organizations that offer a new role to an old leader provide a priceless opportunity for a respected member of the team. One of my chief motivations for working on my own succession plan for almost five years before implementation had to do with watching colleagues in leadership positions in the nonprofit sector stay too long, often because they had difficulty accepting their next, new role on the team. Observing old-guard leaders dragged off the stage kicking and screaming frightened me about my own reaction to ramping down into some sort of retirement. At CitySquare, I had the benefit of plenty of time to plan and roll out the process. By the time we flipped the switch to new leadership and new structure, I was eager to see it happen. My successor had worked hard and effectively to prove himself to the team. We all settled into and embraced our new roles. I even laid out my next five years of objectives! We took good care to communicate as clearly as possible about everything. Dr. John Siburt stepped up from a productive two-year acclimation process within the organization and into the dual role of president (a role I turned over to him) and chief operations officer, while I assumed the supportive role of chief executive officer. My new job finds me working to support and contribute to our team vision that John largely sets, raise funding, and turn outward to the community we serve and depend upon for support. We've both embraced our roles, and it works.

Not Devoting the Time to the Process

Many organizations stumble on leadership transfer because they don't take the time necessary to execute the process. Many boards of directors find it easier to kick the proverbial can down the road when it comes to decision-making concerning the next generation of leadership development and identification. The process, if done correctly, is time consuming. Many delay and procrastinate, setting their organizations up for turmoil and even decline. Time and resources spent on planning, well in advance of the crucial and inevitable shift, will be among the best expenditures you ever decide to make. Map out your plan. Identify candidates. Communicate clearly and thoroughly, again and again. Take your time. Implement your plan. Build in evaluation. Don't be afraid to check in on how everyone involved is doing.

The timeline for our succession seemed about right. John and I met monthly for two years before he joined our team in program management. As he steadily worked himself into roles of increasing responsibility in the organization, we set a date for the key transition. As it turned out, he performed so well that we set the succession date up by one year. Since our reorganization, John and I meet weekly to compare notes and debrief. I've assumed responsibility for arranging a meeting every quarter or so to check in with him on my performance in view of his goals and objectives. If I'm failing to perform to his expectations, I want to know so that I can make corrections.

What's to Hand Off?

When a leadership change takes place through a process of planned succession, personal relationships, organizational history, knowledge of funding sources, strategic understanding, and organizational restructuring must be addressed. A founding or long-time leader makes an essential and beneficial contribution to the organization by working hard at transferring as many of these resources as possible. Friendships and alliances crafted during years of service and personal familiarity must be managed creatively so that the new leader can pick up right where her predecessor left off. Retiring leaders must assume the role of "chief connector" as they serve out this important next and final stage of service to their teams.

Leaders who play games with these crucial assets do their organizations a great disservice and potentially much harm. Passing along introductions and providing guidance about potential resources, human and capital, constitutes one of the essential roles of the departing leader. The heart of the leader emerges for all to see as this process unfolds. The leader who willingly and enthusiastically transfers hard-won assets to her successor performs some of her most essential work. The overall career performance of any leader, especially one who has held leadership positions for long periods of time, can be gauged by how effectively she hands over the reins to the next generation. There is real and amazing joy in handing off every last bit of the resource base that you may have worked for decades building. The experience of seeing your successor receive these essential connections, partners, relationships, and prospects from your hands provides an essential piece to the puzzle of your own personal mission and its essential, enduring meaning. At no point in a person's life work is its true nature and motivation more clearly revealed than in such transitions of power and authority. When the time comes for a clean and effective handoff, excellent leaders don't drop the baton, nor do they make it hard for their teammates to receive the responsibility for the next leg in the organization's race.

Your Turn

1. Recall a situation of leadership succession in which you were involved in some manner. Turn your experience into a story that sums up the major aspects of the experience.
2. What have you learned about leadership succession so far in your own work? How can what you've learned help you if and when you find yourself in a similar situation?
3. What do you think is or would be the most challenging dimension of turning over leadership to another person after you've worked for an extended period of time as the leader?
4. What do you feel would make the experience easier and more productive for you? Explain.
5. What can be a productive role for a board of directors in the process of leadership succession? Why do you say that?

LAGNIAPPE

Living in Louisiana taught me many useful things. One of the most interesting concepts I encountered was "lagniappe" (lan'yap), the custom and habit of throwing in a little extra in most transactions. Like the thirteenth donut in a box of hot pastries. Something you consider gratis. So consider what follows as lagniappe just for you.

Over the years, many people have asked for a summary of my operating philosophy. I am pleased to provide a summation of many of the truths that have shaped and guided my work for more than forty years. Most of these principles became clear to me as I worked closely with the community. As a matter of fact, the closer to the community, the more robust the philosophy forming my plans for action.

In my view, the philosophy you adopt determines the measurable outcomes you will realize. In essence, the various aspects of our operating philosophy serve as building blocks for our community and for real, sustainable community renewal. Clearly, forging a cogent operating philosophy assumes a position of extreme importance to any organization expecting to deliver great results. Consider these principles that define our operational strategies.

> We believe in the ability of people to solve their own problems
> when given access to opportunity and resources.

I've witnessed this again and again in my work in inner city Dallas. People are smart, motivated, and eager to succeed when given the opportunities they need to make progress. If we add capital resources or material assets to the equation, big things result. This is true for low-income neighbors, for nonprofit and for-profit organizations, and for almost any human organizing effort. Most people know what to do to make life better for themselves and their constituencies if they are given a legitimate chance to be successful. Teams that fail in business often reflect in the aftermath about "what might have been" had adequate resources been made available at crucial strategic and tactical pinch points. Tenacity, perseverance, creativity, and vision reside in virtually every group. Successful leaders recognize and nurture these raw assets for the good of their endeavors.

> We believe the resources within a community are adequate
> to initiate genuine renewal and redevelopment.

This follows logically from the previous principle. Recognizing the resident capacity of a target community is essential to success and advancement. The resources of which I speak here are not normally acknowledged because too often they are not regarded as real and vital resources. Street cred cannot be overvalued. Understanding an environment deeply and personally will be essential to any progress. Social capital and identity alignment will aid in the transformation of communities, companies, and campuses. Everyone arrives with some talent, which, if focused and contributed, can assist in the work of renewal and enhanced community health and well-being. Indigenous leaders possess the necessary social capital, neighborhood understandings, and community savvy, often off the charts, to begin the vital work of renewal and restoration. Success remains elusive if both outside and inside resources aren't aligned against the complicated challenges of restoring life to troubled, neglected communities.

> We devote ourselves to the discovery and mobilization of individual and community resources and capacities, many of which we leverage into the work we do from the outside.

As noted already, in most cases, efforts and organizations emerge from the knowledge and resources resident in the community or organizations about which we are concerned. At the same time, we work hard on identifying and delivering outside resources to the community, organization, or specific project. Inherent community and/or organizational resources get things going. Outside capital enables the target community to multiply its own essential assets with missions that respond to community issues and needs. Capitalization precedes and remains essential to progress and to accomplishing the agreed upon mission. The human wealth of the community finds new power for working the community agenda effectively when the benefit of outside assets are made available. However, it is important to realize that the outside financial resources always will be attracted and invested because of the primary, resident social capital of the community or organization in question. Often, we find outside resources allow real solutions to be taken to scale.

> We believe in partnership and collaboration, and therefore we hold all the resources at our disposal with an open hand.

"Collaborate or Die!" assumes the status of primary organizational mantra. Remaining open to partnerships that give and take for the progress of the mission proves essential to delivering on the promise and the identity of our organization. Frankly, I cannot imagine engaging in any undertaking without valued, proven partners (see Chapter Sixteen). In discussions about partnerships, invariably you'll encounter leaders who resist the obvious wisdom of partnerships. Feeling a need to control every aspect of an organization plays into the development of this lethal partnership resistance. The leader who can enter discussions about collaboration with an open, creative, and receptive mind and attitude will quickly begin to measure real gains. The pace, complexity, and difficulty of most enterprise today argues strongly for finding diligent and committed partners to join you in your work. I'm always amazed at the positive energy and the feel good emotions when our organizations strike good, win-win deals among good partners. This ability, forged in a bias toward reciprocity, trust, and delivering the intended results, explains most of whatever success we've enjoyed across the years.

> **We believe racial reconciliation is a prerequisite for genuine community renewal.**

As an organization, CitySquare's mission drives us toward reconciliation in communities, especially across the racial divides our national history perpetuates. Income inequality exemplifies the "new Jim Crow" at work in communities. Until we eliminate racism from our teams, our neighborhoods, our businesses, our educational institutions, and our houses of faith, our work will not be complete. As a people, we remained trapped by the injustices of the United States' apartheid history. Facing the role race plays in our everyday lives is a beginning. We've learned that honest conversation, debate, painstaking storytelling, and emotional catharsis are essential aspects of the anti-racism protocol necessary for teams and organizations desiring to face and overcome the insidious, evil power of racism. It is easy to cast the problems of racism in economic terms. We often hear, "Our problems today have little to do with race and prejudice. Our problems today are all about poverty and economic strength." The problem is that when we scratch the surface of that argument, we find a racial and racist basis for economic disparity. Disproportionate numbers of black and brown people struggle with poverty. Often that poverty is deep and multigenerational. In my view, organizations of all kinds need to adopt a firm corporate commitment, based on the most important company values, to fight and to overcome racism in our culture and national life.

As your team sails directly into these troubled and troubling waters, be prepared for rocky times that guarantee to shock your comfortable world. Embrace the hard knocks, the surprising lessons, and the tears of pain and relief that accompany invaluable breakthroughs of truth and understanding. Teams flourish in multicultural environments. Learn to translate the various cultures within your organization's framework. Commit yourself to understand as deeply as possible the world and the worldviews of your teammates of other races. Likely, we don't need more "sensitivity training." What we need is the ability to speak each other's cultural/social language as a real demonstration of our commitment to love, respect, know, and value every team member.

> We believe that our faith will always lead us
> into the community around us.

Clearly, this is just who we are and choose to be. While it may not be your space, it would have been disingenuous for me to have omitted it from this list. Our faith does not impose itself on others. While the work we accomplish in the community and the services we offer do not expect nor require acceptance of or adherence to our faith values, it is faith that motivates and drives our action.

Within our organization, we find extremely diverse faith expressions, including "none." Those of us motivated and shaped by faith regularly experience a clear movement toward the community. In fact, our faith drives us into the community, where we discover the formative outlines and the locus of our most important work. This is who we are and have been from the beginning at CitySquare. So while I understand that this is not the position, philosophy, or reality for all teams or organizations, it is ours. Faith motivates the work we do and the actions we take.

> We accept people where we find them, and, as friendships develop, we work to engage human potential with new opportunity.

We fancy ourselves "urban concierges" devoted to high-energy customer service. Whether working the streets, the classrooms, the bars, or the businesses of our community, we show up with a deep, instilled commitment to high-touch, transformative service and friendship. No one forces anything on anyone in our organization. That said, we stand at the ready to engage every neighbor in achieving the personal goals each decides to pursue. In our society, we vastly underappreciate the power of expressing and acting out of genuine concern for others. Friendship delivers medicinal benefits beyond our ability to measure completely. As previously noted, in his important book *Chasing the Scream: The First and Last Days of the War on Drugs*, Johann Hari demonstrates that the causes and cures of drug addiction relate more to robust human connections and bonding as friends than to chemical addiction.[1] We have certainly observed this phenomenon in our work with addicts in the inner city. The power of community connections cannot be overemphasized. Friendship contains amazing power to make life work for customers and teams.

As a leader, the culture you inspire should include absolute intolerance of people who do not and cannot love and respect everyone who moves in and out of the world of your organization. Friendship is so basic to our enterprise. Without it, we most certainly fail.

> We believe "re-neighboring" will be an important part
> of community development and renewal.

Moving into a target neighborhood provides a level of credibility to organizational leaders who choose to take this decisive, distinguishing step. When leaders and team members relocate to the community of interest, they cast a vote for the neighborhood and the neighbors residing there. Deliberate relocation provides a depth of identification few if any other actions can hope to achieve. Moving into the challenged community fast-forwards the process of acceptance for those who come to stay and who remain to become an authentic part of the community fabric. As a result, a number of our team will always live in the communities where we work. Not everyone should feel compelled to move to an inner city neighborhood, for example, in order to work in an organization whose mission is urban renewal. Relocation should not be required or forced upon team members. However, as leaders move closer to the communities of interest to their organizations, credibility and acceptance levels only increase.

> We believe typical charity must be replaced by
> compassionate community building as a basic strategy.

Classic charity tends to cripple its long-term recipients. Charity tends to produce unhealthy dependence. Charity produces "feel good" experiences for volunteers and an expanding "service project" institutional response. Charity alone seldom, if ever, contributes to lasting community restoration.

As a result, we believe that relief efforts, while at times essential and necessary in emergencies, must be accompanied by building healthy communities whose members seldom need charity to survive. Times can become so harsh and tentative that groups feel the urgency to pour in large amounts of charitable resources. But such efforts must not be allowed to replace the equally urgent demands to build vibrant communities that learn to care for their own weak and broken members. Sadly, charity sometimes blocks the efforts of organizations determined to build new communities while offering stronger opportunity and options for people. Charity seldom challenges or changes the status quo. Charity can grow organizational efficiencies (I call this the "straight pantry shelved canned corn" phenomenon). Charity alone, if it persists, cannot build or renew communities. Community building takes us in the direction of renewed health, wellness, and economic development to the end that charity is rare and delivered only in emergency situations.

> We believe for community to thrive, the institutions that make healthy communities possible must be renewed and strengthened.

Included in any list of the primary institutions necessary for community health would be home, school, business, health, public safety, governments, and communities of faith. Leaders seeking to get things done in, with, and for communities will find as many ways as possible to work for the strengthening of these fundamentally important institutions. Often, I hear counsel that urges us as an organization to focus on just one thing rather than attempting to do so many different things. That approach may work in widget manufacturing or in product marketing and sales, but in the nonprofit sector concerned for community restoration and the curtailment of poverty, rifle-shot approaches don't work as well as one might think. Willing coalitions employing a broad-based frontal assault on poverty as the common enemy will outperform more singular, narrow-focused efforts. Institutional renewal should be among our primary tactics as we apply clear strategies to overcome poverty and its cruel effects on our communities.

We believe the public, private, faith, and community-based organizations of a city must all play important roles in community redevelopment.

To build strong communities, no one segment or interest group of a city or neighborhood will possess adequate resources to get the job done. Community efforts to ignite new life achieve success most consistently when a wide variety of players put "skin in the game." From the customers of a food relief center to the city manager who crafts multibillion dollar annual budgets; from the small congregation of worshippers to the high steeple, regional churches; and from the charitable foundations to the largest corporation in town—we include everyone in the battle to improve communities for the good of all.

We believe it is better to teach a girl to fish than to give her a fish; however, best of all is pond ownership.

This is not a novel or new idea in the main. Obviously, developing skills lead to deepening self-sufficiency and broad life change. When a person receives the necessary skills to work at a higher level of proficiency, that person no longer needs to depend upon charitable relief efforts or public assistance. Even better than enhanced skills is the increased opportunity and responsibility of owning the source of one's wealth. This operating principle grows more important with each passing day. Income and net worth inequity present huge challenges to our nation. Our current economic situation, especially as revealed in analyzing the ever-expanding wealth gap, appears unsustainable. Driven by an equally onerous skills gap, the difficulty of wealth accumulation and social mobility for certain segments of our population threaten to drive even deeper divisions into the heart of our national life. Working on the creation of economic and educational systems leading to equitable sharing of the wealth in return for hard work, ingenuity, and personal sacrifice must become a top priority for the nation, and more particularly for organizations focused on poverty alleviation and the forces that conspire to block people from genuine opportunity and wealth building.

Leaders intent on finding new approaches for closing the income gap in the nation should devote themselves to fully understanding the economic trends and the rich store of available data regarding the very real challenges presented by generational poverty and the resulting wealth gap. Creating programmatic and pragmatic responses to the real challenge of cultivating opportunities, skills, and pathways to property or "pond" ownership may represent the most difficult work facing leaders today, as well as the most effective way to close the staggering wealth gap while renewing communities.

> We believe in the value of both chaos and ownership.

This principle always causes people, including devoted team members, to stop, cringe, and start asking questions. But the notions here remain solid.

Ownership is hard enough to grasp as we face the consequences of low skills and wages set alongside the almost impossible goal of owning anything leading to the creation of real wealth. Still, most people get the point of ownership's importance. Then there is the importance of "buy in" to community restoration efforts. If the community cannot be sold, if they don't feel an ownership stake in whatever the deal, you can forget about impact. Leaders will commit to inviting everyone into the work and life of the organizations they direct. The essential outcome? Ownership. Ownership that makes the community work and the world go around. Never underestimate its importance. Never shortchange your team or your community by under-investing in the spread of as many owners as possible. Recognize just how important ownership is in bringing the correct players together to affect change in a community.

So, what about chaos (see Chapter Seventeen)? Chaos always allows plenty of room for lively faith. Chaos also forces people to count on one another. This somewhat forced dependency emerges from the perceived threat and the simple swirl caused by times of real chaos. Effective leaders learn the dance of disruption. On one occasion, I heard renowned business leader and author Tom Peters say, "If it's not broke, break it!" That may sound foolhardy, but there come times in every organization when the only way through crippling paralysis is bold, disruptive action. Changing the assignments of key players on your team may create renewing tension and enhanced attention to new details. Discontinuing long-running programs and replacing them with highly innovative initiatives involving some measure of risk can bring a sense of excitement and renewal to fatigued players. The benefits of the chaos of disruption are seldom an easy sell. However, almost always, after the fact of implementing the new direction, renewing energy descends on teams that embrace the new way with enthusiasm and vision.

Of course, chaos often arrives without an invitation! Whether intentional, as in leader-induced disruption, or the chaos that attacks us in an unplanned crisis of sweeping dimensions, these experiences call for faith. Chaos leaves room for trusting outside ourselves and our own limitations. No matter how hard or frightening, chaos usually delivers new strength to leaders and fresh incentive to their teams.

Your Turn

1. What is one question provoked by the principles of this operating philosophy? Explain why you would ask this.
2. How do you feel about chaos? How do chaotic situations affect you as a leader? Can you provide an example?
3. How important is "ownership" in the group process? Why?
4. What ideas do you have about increasing "pond ownership" as you do your work?
5. What are your ideas and questions about the notion of "re-neighboring" inner city communities?
6. How do you react to the idea that communities have the capital they need to begin community renewal? How can that be possible?

NOTE

[1] Johann Hari, *Chasing the Scream: The First and Last Days of the War on Drugs* (New York: Bloomsbury, 2016), Kindle.

SUGGESTED READING

Electronic news media people depend on creative "B-roll" capture in order to tell their stories. What follows constitutes reading
that you might call my "background music" or "B-Roll" as I do
my work and as I continue to be a student of the inner city and of
poverty. I gladly commend each entry to your exploration!

⚬ ⚬ ⚬ ⚬ ⚬ ⚬ 〰 ⚬ ⚬ ⚬ ⚬ ⚬ ⚬

Allen, Jimmy. *Burden of a Secret: A Story of Truth and Mercy in The Face of AIDS*. Nashville, TN: Moorings, 1995.

Anderson, Jon Lee. *Che Guevara: A Revolutionary Life*. New York: Grove Press, 1997.

Angus, Jeff. *Management by Baseball: The Official Rules for Winning Management in Any Field*. New York: HarperCollins, 2006.

Barboza, Steven, ed. *The African American Book of Values*. New York: Doubleday, 1998.

Brands, H. W. *Traitor to His Class: The Privileged Life and Radical Presidency of Franklin Delano Roosevelt*. New York: Anchor Books, 2008.

Brian, Barry. *Why Social Justice Matters*. Malden, MA: Polity Press, 2005.

Brueggemann, Walter. *The Prophetic Imagination*. Minneapolis, MN: Fortress Press, 2001.

Brunner, Emil. *Faith, Hope, and Love*. Philadelphia, PA: The Westminster Press, 1956.

Collins, Jim. *Built to Last: Successful Habits of Visionary Companies*. New York: Harper Business Essentials, 1994.

———. *Good to Great: Why Some Companies Make the Leap and Others Don't*. New York: Harper Business, 2001.

———. *Good to Great and the Social Sectors*. Boulder, CO: Jim Collins, 2005.

Chrysostom, John. *On Wealth and Poverty*. Crestwood, NY: St. Vladimir's Seminary Press, 1981.

Coates, Ta-Nehisi. *Between the World and Me*. New York: Spiegel and Grau, 2015.

Cone, James H. *Black Theology & Black Power*. New York: The Seabury Press, 1969.

———. *A Theology of Black Liberation*. Maryknoll, NY: Orbis Books, 1997.

Cone, James H., and Gayraud S. Wilmore. *Black Theology: A Documentary History, 1966-1979*. Maryknoll, NY: Orbis Books, 1979.

Conrad, Joseph. *Heart of Darkness*. New York: Penguin Books, 1989.

Crutchfield, Leslie R., and Heather McLeod Grant. *Forces for Good: The Six Practices of High-Impact Nonprofits*. San Francisco, CA: Jossey-Bass, 2008.

Dalrymple, Theodore. *Life at The Bottom: The Worldview That Makes the Underclass*. Chicago: Ivan R. Dee, 2001.

de Mello, Anthony. *Awareness: The Perils and Opportunities of Reality*. New York: Image Books, 1990.

Desmond, Matthew. *Evicted: Poverty and Profit in the American City*. New York: Crown Publishers, 2016.

Ellsberg, Robert, ed. *The Duty of Delight: The Diaries of Dorothy Day*. Milwaukee, WI: Marquette University Press, 2008.

Fernandez-Armesto, Felipe. *Our America: A Hispanic History of the United States*. New York: W. W. Norton, 2014.

Freiberg, Kevin and Jackie. *Guts! Companies That Blow the Doors Off Business-As-Usual*. New York: Currency Book, 2004.

Friedman, Thomas L. *The World Is Flat: A Brief History of the Twenty-First Century*. New York: Farrar, Straus & Giroux, 2005.

———. *Hot, Flat, and Crowded: Why We Need A Revolution—And How It Can Renew America*. New York: Farrar, Straus & Giroux, 2008.

Glaeser, Edward. *Triumph of the City: How Our Greatest Invention Makes Us Richer, Smarter, Greener, Healthier, and Happier*. New York: The Penguin Press, 2011.

Glassman, Bernard, and Rick Fields. *Instructions to the Cook: A Zen Master's Lessons in Living a Life That Matters.* New York: Bell Tower, 1996.

Goldstone, Lawrence. *Inherently Unequal: The Betrayal of Equal Rights by the Supreme Court, 1865-1903.* New York: Walker & Company, 2011.

Hari, Johann. *Chasing the Scream: The First and Last Days of the War on Drugs.* New York: Bloomsbury, 2016.

Halberstam, David. *The Children.* New York: Random House, 1998.

———. *The Teammates: A Portrait of a Friendship.* New York: Hyperion, 2003.

Hamill, Susan Pace. *The Least of These: Fair Taxes and the Moral Duty of Christians.* Birmingham, AL: Sweetwater Press, 2003.

Hanlon, Joseph, Armando Barrientos, and David Hulme. *Just Give Money to the Poor: The Development Revolution from the Global South.* Sterling, VA: Kumarian Press, 2010.

Jackson, Phil. *Eleven Rings: The Soul of Success.* New York: The Penguin Press, 2013.

Kaplan, Saul. *The Business Model Innovation Factory: How to Stay Relevant When the World Is Changing.* Hoboken, NJ: John Wiley and Sons, Inc., 2012.

Katz, Bruce, and Jennifer Bradley. *The Metropolitan Revolution: How Cities and Metros Are Fixing Our Broken Politics and Fragile Economy.* Washington, DC: Brookings Institution Press, 2013.

Kimmel, Michael. *Angry White Men: American Masculinity at the End of An Era.* New York: Nation Books, 2013.

Kotkin, Joel. *The City: A Global History.* New York: Modern Library, 2005.

Kozol, Jonathan. *Illiterate America.* New York: Penguin Books, 1985.

———. *Amazing Grace: The Lives of Children and the Conscience of a Nation.* New York: Crown Publishers, 1995.

———. *Ordinary Resurrections: Children in the Years of Hope.* New York: Crown Publishers, 2000.

———. *The Shames of the Nation: The Restoration of Apartheid Schooling in America.* New York: Crown Publishers, 2005.

Kretzmann, John P., and John L. McKnight. *Building Communities from the Inside Out: A Path Toward Finding and Mobilizing a Community's Assets.* Chicago: ACTA Publications, 1993.

Kristof, Nicholas D., and Sheryl WuDunn. *A Path Appears: Transforming Lives, Creating Opportunity.* New York: Alfred A. Knopf, 2014.

———. *Half Sky: Turning Oppression into Opportunity For Women Worldwide.* New York: Vintage House, 2009.

Lee, Bill. *The Hidden Wealth of Customers: Realizing the Untapped Value of Your Most Important Asset*. Boston: Harvard Business Review Press, 2012.

Lencioni, Patrick. *The Five Dysfunctions of a Team: A Leadership Fable*. San Francisco, CA: Jossey-Bass, 2002.

Levine, Philip. *What Work Is: Poems*. New York: Alfred A. Knopf, 2007.

Lewis, David Levering. *W. E. B. DuBois: Biography of a Race, 1868-1919*. New York: Henry Holt, 1993.

Mackey, John, and Raj Sisodia. *Conscious Capitalism: Liberating the Heroic Spirit of Business*. Boston: Harvard Business Review Press, 2013.

Marable, Manning. *Malcolm X: A Life of Reinvention*. New York: Viking Press, 2011.

Moreton, Bethany. *To Serve God and Wal-Mart: The Making of Christian Free Enterprise*. Cambridge, MA: Harvard University Press, 2009.

Mullainathan, Sendhill, and Eldar Shatir. *Scarcity: Why Having Too Little Means So Much*. New York: Time Books, 2013.

Murphy, Liam, and Thomas Nagel. *The Myth of Ownership: Taxes and Justice*. New York: Oxford University Press, 2002.

Naim, Moises. *The End of Power: From Boardrooms to Battlefields and Churches to States, Why Being in Charge Isn't What It Used to Be*. New York: Basic Books, 2013.

Nelson, Jack A. *Hunger for Justice: The Politics of Food and Faith*. Maryknoll, NY: Orbis Books, 1986.

Newport, Cal. *Deep Work: Rules for Focused Success in a Distracted World*. New York: Grand Central Publishing, 2016.

Niebuhr, Reinhold. *The Nature and Destiny of Man* (Vol. 1 Human Nature). New York: Scribner's, 1941.

———. *The Nature and Destiny of Man* (Vol. 2 Human Destiny). New York: Scribner's, 1943.

Obama, Barack. *The Audacity of Hope: Thoughts on Reclaiming the American Dream*. New York: Crown Publishers, 2006.

Orwell, George. *Why I Write*. New York: Penguin Books, 2004.

Palmer, Parker J. *Let Your Life Speak: Listening for the Voice of Vocation*. New York: Jossey-Bass, 1999.

Painter, Nell Irvin. *The History of White People*. New York: W. W. Norton, 2010.

Parks, Rosa, with Gregory J. Reed. *Quiet Strength*. Grand Rapids, MI: Zondervan Publishing House, 1994.

Perkins, John M. *Beyond Charity: The Call to Christian Community Development*. Grand Rapids, MI.: Baker Books, 1993.

Peters, Tom. *The Circle of Innovation: You Can't Shrink Your Way to Greatness*. New York: Vintage Books, 1997.

Peters, Tom. *Thriving on Chaos: Handbook for a Management Revolution*. New York: Alfred A. Knopf, Inc., 1987.

Phillips, Donald. *Martin Luther King, Jr. on Leadership*. New York: Warner Books, 1998.

Phillips, Kevin. *Wealth and Democracy: A Political History of the American Rich*. New York: Broadway Books, 2002.

Phillips, Michael. *White Metropolis: Race, Ethnicity and Religion in Dallas, 1841-2001*. Austin, TX: University of Texas Press, 2002.

Powell, Lawrence N. *The Accidental City: Improvising New Orleans*. Cambridge, MA: Harvard University Press, 2012.

Prahalad, C. K. *The Fortune at the Bottom of the Pyramid: Eradicating Poverty through Profits*. Upper Saddle River, NJ: Wharton School Publishing, 2005.

Rothstein, Richard. *The Color of Law: A Forgotten History of How Our Government Segregated America*. New York: Liversight Publishing Corporation, 2017.

Rauschenbusch, Walter. *A Theology for The Social Gospel*. New York: The Macmillan Company, 1918.

Sachs, Jeffrey D. *The End of Poverty: Economic Possibilities for Our Time*. New York: The Penguin Press, 2005.

Sagawa, Shirley. *The Charismatic Organization: 8 Ways to Grow a Nonprofit That Builds Buzz, Delights Donors, and Energizes Employees*. San Francisco, CA: Jossey-Bass, 2009.

Schroeder, Alice. *The Snowball: Warren Buffett and the Business of Life*. New York: Bantam Books, 2008.

Schutze, Jim. *The Accommodation: The Politics of Race in an American City*. New York: Citadel Press, 1987.

Schweitzer, Albert. *The Quest of the Historical Jesus*. New York: The Macmillan Company, 1956.

Segal, Ronald. *The Black Diaspora: Five Centuries of the Black Experience Outside Africa*. New York: Farrar, Straus & Giroux, 1995.

Shipler, David K. *The Working Poor: Invisible in America*. New York: Vintage Books, 2005.

Shulman, Beth. *The Betrayal of Work: How Low-Wage Jobs Fail 30 Million Americans*. New York: The New Press, 2003.

Stevenson, Bryan. *Just Mercy: A Story of Injustice and Redemption*. New York: Spiegel & Grau, 2014.

Sutton, Robert I. *The No Asshole Rule: Building a Civilized Workplace and Surviving One That Isn't*. New York: Business Plus, 2007.

Tagore, Rabindranath, ed. *The Heart of God: Prayers of Rabindranath Tagore*. North Clarendon, VT: Tuttle Publishing, 2004.

Takaki, Ronald. *A Different Mirror: A History of Multicultural America*. Revised Edition. New York: Back Bay Books, 1993.

Theoharis, Jeanne. *The Rebellious Life of Mrs. Rosa Parks*. Boston: Beacon Press, 2013.

Vallely, Paul. *Pope Francis: The Struggle for the Soul of Catholicism*. New York: Bloomsbury, 2015.

West, Cornel. *Race Matters*. New York: Vintage Books, 1994.

Willink, Jocko, and Leif Babin. *Extreme Ownership: How U.S. Navy Seals Lead and Win*. New York: St. Martin's Press, 2015.

Wolters, Clifton, trans. *The Cloud of Unknowing*. Baltimore, MD: Penguin Books, 1961.

Woodward, C. Vann. *The Strange Career of Jim Crow*. Third Revised Version. New York: Oxford University Press, 1974.

Wright, Lawrence. *In the New World: Growing Up with America, 1960-1984*. New York: Alfred A. Knopf, 1988.

Yunus, Muhammad. *Building Social Business: The New Kind of Capitalism That Serves Humanity's Most Pressing Needs*. New York: Public Affairs, 2010.

Zinn, Howard. *A People's History of the United States*. New York: HarperCollins Publishers, 1995.